I Met Paul VI

I Met Paul VI

The Pope by Those Who Knew Him

Rino Fisichella

Translated by
Daniel B. Gallagher

Gracewing

Ho incontrato Paolo VI, La sua santità dalla voce dei testimoni
© 2014 Edizioni San Paolo s.r.l.
Piazza Soncino 5
20092 Cinisello Balsamo (Milano)
ITALIA
www.edizionisanpaolo.it

First published in England in 2016
by
Gracewing
2 Southern Avenue
Leominster
Herefordshire HR6 0QF
United Kingdom
www.gracewing.co.uk

ISBN 978 085244 900 4

Typeset by Gracewing

Cover design by Bernardita Peña Hurtado

Contents

INTRODUCTION

HE NAME AND person of Paul VI are closely linked to the Second Vatican Council. Granted, it was Pope John XXIII's prophetic vision that initially conceived this historic event that left an indelible mark on the Church and the world in the twentieth century. But it is equally true that bringing the Council to its favorable conclusion and leading the Church in the first steps of its implementation required a personality like Montini's. He, more than anyone else at that pivotal moment in history, had the wherewithal to enact such an ambitious and far-reaching program for the Church's renewal as Vatican II. Indeed, the entire span of Paul VI's Pontificate was marked by the renewal of the Church indicated by the Council.

The present book is not a biography of Paul VI. Plenty of detailed studies of his person and Pontificate have been written by professional historians over the years. To these we can add several notable studies of his teaching as Archbishop of Milan and the Successor of Peter. The present volume is rather a description of the results of his cause for beatification.

Not everyone may be familiar with the process of beatification and canonization. When a believer shows signs of holiness by living the Gospel in a heroic way, his or her cause can be taken up a few years after death to allow for a wider recognition of his or her holiness throughout the Church. The process of beatification is a "trial" in a true sense, involving judges and witnesses, by which the holiness of life and Christian merits of the individual are ascertained. The first stage of the process usually takes place in the diocese where the candidate died. An expert, called a postulator, asks the diocesan bishop to initiate the process and to collect the "acts," or rather the necessary material, to conduct the process and to maintain a proper record of the cause's progress. Once these steps have been completed, the cause is forwarded to the Congregation for the Causes of Saints at the Vatican. This is the office responsible for reviewing the procedural acts. If there are no obstacles, a relator takes over for the postulator and redacts what is called a *positio*. The *positio* is simply a synthesized version of the acts of the cause containing biographical information, especially a description of how he or she lived out the theological virtues of faith, hope, and love, in addition to the cardinal virtues of prudence, justice, fortitude, and temperance. At this point a transcription is made of the witnesses' testimony, favorable and unfavorable, carried out at the diocesan level, as well as objective data needed to confirm the procedural conclusions. The *positio* is then submitted to professional historians and analyzed by nine consultant theologians whose task it is to evaluate the consistent development of the cause and the objective presence of the virtues in the life of the Servant of God. Once this phase is completed, if the consulters have reached a positive conclusion regarding the validity of the cause, the *positio* is sent, together with the votes of the consultant theologians, for the ultimate consideration of the Congregation.

An ordinary session of the Congregation's cardinals and bishops is convened to pass final judgment on the cause. One of the "judges" is designated to be *ponens*.

His job is to study the entire cause in order to present it synthetically to the members of the Congregation so that they may more effectively arrive at a decision. The session concludes with a vote, which is then presented to the pope who, should he deem it opportune, will acknowledge the candidate's virtues. At this point the Servant of God is declared "Venerable". Then, in order to proceed to beatification, at least one miracle is necessary. This paves the way to a second process. As in the previous phase, all objective proof is collected, especially that of a medical nature or that based on personal experience, so as to determine whether the phenomenon is inexplicable by modern-day science. It is a complex and delicate process. In addition to witness testimony, medical specialists are commissioned to verify directly the alleged healing. These physicians are referred to as experts *ab inspectione*. Once their positive vote is obtained, all the medical documentation is forwarded to the Congregation for the Causes of Saints, which then submits it to the Congregation's Medical Commission, usually composed of seven appointed specialists. Upon completion of their work, these are called to express their opinion on four questions: on the diagnosis of the illness, the prognosis, the treatment, and on the various ways the healing could have occurred. More specifically, the medical specialists must profess whether the healing has a scientific explanation or whether, at present, science has no way of accounting for the healing. If they give a positive vote, the testimony of witnesses is then collected. These witnesses must confirm that the miracle occurred exclusively through the intercession of the Venerable in question. The results of this phase are then submitted for the consideration of the theologian consultants. If they issue a favorable vote, the entire cause is taken up again by an ordinary session of the cardinals and bishops of the Congregation. A *relator*—usually, but not necessarily, the same person who performed this role during the examination of virtues—is chosen to present the details surrounding the miracle. Once this is done, the *ponens* asks for the vote of the cardinals and bishops. After deliberations, their vote is sent to the pope for his final stamp of approval on the beatification. The process is basically the same for canonization, except that the deliberations are focused simply on one more miracle attributable to the Blessed. The difference between a Blessed and a Saint is also determined by the kind of "cult" or veneration the Church wishes to attribute to the individual. While for a Blessed the cult is limited to a local Church, for a Saint the cult is proposed to the universal Church.

This brief *excursus* is necessary to help the reader understand the material presented in the following chapters. I was selected to serve as *ponens* for the cause of Pope Paul IV. This was an enormous honor and a grace for me. Paul VI was the pope of my youth, my priestly formation, and my first years of priestly ministry at the parish of the Holy Roman Protomartyrs in the Diocese of Rome. I was present at many public audiences given by His Holiness on various occasions. But the first time I met him personally was at the Synod on Evangelization. I was asked to help with the work of the Synod, and at the end of the sessions the Pope gave his usual greeting to all the bishops and their collaborators. When my turn arrived I knelt before him. His gaze was fixed sharply on my face. His words of appreciation and thanks will forever remain etched in my mind. After I was ordained a deacon, the then-Master of Ceremonies, Msgr Virgilio Noè, called me at least three times to perform diaconal services at papal Masses. The last time occurred a few weeks before my priestly ordination in March of 1976. At this particular Eucharist, the Pope looked exhausted and weak. Msgr Noè told His Holiness at the end of Mass that I would be ordained to the priesthood within a few days. The Pope's tense face immediately relaxed. He broke out into a sincere, cordial, fatherly smile and exclaimed: "What wonderful news!" He then extended his hand, blessed me on the head, saying, *"Sit odor vitae tuae delectamentum Ecclesiae Christi."* "May the fragrance of your life be a joy for Christ's Church ." With these words, taken from the venerable Church Fathers, Pope Paul VI entrusted me with the enormous task that lay ahead.

In the early morning of August 7th, just as we were concluding a session of the youth summer camp at Ollomont in the mountains of Val d'Aosta, Fabio returned breathless from the village bearing news of the pope's death the previous evening. I was immediately thrown into a state of confusion. The pope of my youth had died!

The entrustment of his cause to my care presented me with a blessed opportunity to get to know the man even better. I became more familiar with him through the testimony of those who had been closest to him. The things they talked about were things of daily life, things which normally escape our attention when it comes to famous people, but things essential when it comes to ascertaining their sanctity. I was offered a glimpse into the personal life of Pope Montini outside the public domain. This allowed me to penetrate the depths of his soul and to see how authentic his personality really was.

The pages that follow are inspired by the process of beatification. I hope they will help many people know better the holiness of a pope who had such an enormous impact on the world in the twentieth century.

1

ONE MAN ALONE

AUL VI WAS elected the 262nd successor to Saint Peter on June 21st, 1963. His predecessor, Saint John XXIII, had inaugurated the 21st Ecumenical Council in the Church's history. It opened with a solemn ceremony in Saint Peter's Basilica on October 11th, 1962. This enormous undertaking of the Church, conceived by the prophetic vision of John XXIII, was suddenly interrupted by his untimely death on June 3rd, 1963, after only one session had been completed. An equally prophetic push was needed to continue the Council and to implement the renewal it called for with a long-term vision. Giovanni Battista Montini was better suited for this than anyone else at the time. His personality and life were characterized by something special: in every event and situation, he perceived a clear call to follow the Lord radically and unconditionally. This capacity for decisive discernment sprang up from an original call he received in 1915. He responded by entering the seminary in Brescia to begin his journey to the priesthood.

One only has to read the pages of his copious writings to see how much his life, especially during the critical years of his Pontificate, developed in the light of that initial call. That call made him faithful and courageous, capable of making difficult and often

unpopular decisions, always solidly anchored in his
priestly vocation. Paul VI's firm grasp of modern
culture, fostered by such teachers and friends as
Jacques Maritain and Etienne Gilson, helped his preparation enormously. He was anything but a rootless
follower of trendy theories that left virtually an entire
generation disillusioned or crushed under the weight
of ideology. To the contrary, he had a sharp, critical
mind. This could only have come from the strength of
a faith penetrating reason and from a first-class theological and philosophical formation, quite rare at the
time. His desire to be familiar with, study, and deeply
enter into the mystery of faith so as to express it in all
its freshness was what most characterized his pastoral
action and intellectual endeavors.

He was indeed a unique person. This was most
evident in the key decisions he had to make as the
successor of Peter: decisions that could not easily be
delegated. One text remains essential for understanding his spirituality and thinking in the wake of his
election to the See of Peter:

> I must be fully conscious now of the position
> and duties that are mine, which characterize me
> and render me inevitably responsible in the
> presence of God, the Church, and humanity. It
> is an entirely unique position to be in. It places
> me in extreme solitude. I was already in a place
> of heavy responsibility, but now it is almost
> overwhelming. It makes me dizzy. I feel like a
> statue on a pedestal, the only differing being
> the statue is alive. I feel like there is nothing and
> no one around me. I must stand on my own,
> work on my own, converse with myself, delib-
> erate and think within the intimate forum of my
> own conscience. If life in community is penance,

this must be all the more so. Even Jesus himself was alone on the cross. In that moment, we heard him converse with God and express his desolation: *Eloi, Eloi* ... Indeed, I should actually feed off this solitude. I must not be afraid. I cannot depend on anything outside myself that would exonerate me from my duty, which is to desire, to choose, and to assume all responsibility, to lead others, even if it seems illogical and absurd. And I must suffer by myself. Consoling reassurances should be far and few: only the depths of my spirit remain for me. Myself and God. My conversation with Him becomes utterly complete and incommunicable.

Texts like this crystallize the meaning of Paul VI's existence. Little by little, he began to understand how difficult and unique the situation is for someone called to make difficult choices that involved the entire Church. The following text makes this clear:

The lamp on the candelabra burns itself out. But it does a function: to give light to others. To everyone, if possible. It holds a unique and solitary position; it performs a public and communitarian function; there is no office comparable to mine in keeping communion with others. *Others.* This mystery toward which I must constantly direct myself, surpassing the mystery of my own individuality or seeming incommunicability. "Others" who are mine and are Christ's. "Others" who are the world. "Others" who *are* Christ. "Others" at whose service I am. That is it: each and every person is my neighbor. How much goodness we need! Every encounter should lead to a revelation. Sympathy for everyone; love toward the world. Universal prayer and love. Always taking on

responsibility for the good of others: *that* is
papal politics! What a heart this requires! A
heart sensitive to every need; a heart ready to
do good at every opportunity; a heart free to
take on poverty willingly; a magnanimous
heart, ready to forgive at any moment, ready
for every reasonable endeavor; a heart tender
to everything delicate; a heart pure for the
nourishment of others…

These words truly echo a life-program, even in the
solitude of a journey requiring only that one abandon
himself to follow: to follow in a way wholly unique to
the Successor of Peter who must obey the Lord's
command to cast one's nets into the sea, certain they
will be filled, but not knowing how or when. In light
of Montini's reflections, the following statement cap-
tures his entire experience: "For me, the spiritual
stature of Paul VI can be summed up in one word: 'the
heart'." These words pave the way to Paul VI's faith
and teaching. They clear up any doubt whether he was
decisive or capable of making hard decisions. To the
contrary, he was motivated by a genuine and fundamental *prudence* to understand the wide range of
complex problems and the repercussions of any of his
decisions. This virtue of prudence sustained him along
with an indescribable charity cutting to the core of his
existence. Paul VI was entirely aware of the importance
of a strong Christian witness, and his life was characterized by this key aspect of his teaching. A phrase
included in the Post-Synodal Exhortation *Evangelii
Nuntiandi* became proverbial in expressing the wisdom
of this truth: "Modern man listens more willingly to
witnesses than to teachers, and if he does listen to
teachers, it is because they are witnesses." (§41)

In short, Paul VI did not simply live according to an inborn characteristic that gave him a natural tendency to be kind and generous toward others. Rather, he turned these personal character traits into a means of following a deliberate path toward holiness. The finesse of soul that characterized much of his behavior — especially toward those who caused great suffering in his life — was a life choice and not merely a natural disposition. This character trait led to unfair judgments about him. But that too manifests only his genuine nobility of soul and universal charity. Msgr G. B. Guzzetti, a priest close to him for many years while Montini was in Milan, was a privileged witness of this.

He certainly had a great love for neighbor and an extreme kindness in dealing with others. He had an air of refinement: he was never able to tell a priest when he was wrong, even to the point of showing a weakness in his ability to command. It was a charity that manifested itself in a clear form of kindness that even bordered on weakness in his ability to make important decisions about people.

It is clear that at the basis of these personal traits one catches a glimpse of the strength of Montini's charity, which for him became a sign of mercy. In short, he had the tendency to correct rather than judge or punish people when they were wrong, especially if they were priests.

It is also worth recalling the memories of a great theologian, Henri de Lubac, with regard to the fifteen years of Paul VI's Pontificate. They appear in the June 20th–21st edition of *l'Osservatore Romano* just a few months before Montini's death. They highlight the enormous impact Pope Paul VI and his teaching had on the Church and would continue to have on future generations. At the same time, they reveal the suffering of a man who had become the target of unfair criticism both inside and outside the Church, simply because he decided to stay firm in his responsibility of remaining a faithful successor to Peter:

> June 1963. One morning, as I was slowly waking up from a foggy state after two successive surgeries, I saw, like a dream, an indistinct shadow leaning over my hospital bed, and I heard two words: "Montini ... Paul VI ...". At that very instant, my long nightmare had ended. Contact with the real world was reestablished. Once more light and life arose for me. Was it a coincidence? Yes, but much more. A great sense of hope began to sweep over me: a hope that could not be disappointed. As heir to John XXIII, Paul VI saw the Council to its completion. Day after day, he promoted its implementation. The Church was once more being renewed. With the reinvigorating wind of Pentecost, the tree of the Cross was again blossoming, promising new fruit. At the same time, however, a storm was brewing once more. Those who blame the Council for this have no idea what they are talking about. One did not have to be a prophet to see the warning signs long before that. The shock, however, would have been less jarring without an immediate cause, a satisfactory explanation of which it is too early to give, but which anxious historians, frantically sifting through documentation, will not have the patience to analyze deeply. The Church was inviting her children to pull together their energies in an atmosphere of freedom. Not everyone knew how to understand it, or they were too worried about trying to make sense of it. In many cases— and this is a fact, as unwelcome as it will be to

many people—the Council was betrayed. Not only because of its natural bent, but because of what we might call a para-Council, just as bad as an anti-Council, an outright opposition, but much more effective. In this sense the fate of the Council is similar to that of the Gospel: I suppose that many were intent on re-reading it in one way or another so that they wouldn't be too embarrassed to preach what it contained. In any case, after fifteen years, Pope Paul is up to the task. Without knowing him, I had learned enough of him to be sure that the Church was going to be in good hands. With steady and tenacious firmness giving rise to an equally tenacious history, he guides the ship. In response to everything that gives fodder to his detractors, one thing alone needs to be kept in mind: the pain that torments him at times is that he cannot remain silent, even if it breaks him or wears away his stamina. Indeed, among the many signs of his humanity, it would be a pity if this were lacking: a trait so similar to Jesus. And what makes it even more special is that this trait is sadly unrecognized and unappreciated by others; not so much by the "world" or by Christians, be they Catholic and non-Catholic, but by those from whom he would have been right to expect much support. Once upon a time there was talk of "court theologians," intellectuals gathered around the Prince. If such theologians are around today, anyone with eyes to see would understand that we don't need to seek them around the Chair of Peter. The omnipotent queen who generously bestows gifts on her subjects is to be found elsewhere. But the Christ who was the victim of abuse is closer to Peter now than ever. It is an absurd and paradoxical

situation. At the very moment when the papacy—stripped of the awkward trappings of a
bygone era—presents itself, after the last
Council, as on the cutting-edge of an evangelical
renewal and redoubles its efforts to bring this
about, sharp voices of opposition are heard
which then fall into a disdainful silence. On the
other hand, rather than from forces outside the
Church or from those unable to comprehend the
Council because of the usual prejudices, it is
from the inside, and especially from those who
have not been faithful to their vocation, that she
is publically scoffed in the person of her primary
Pastor. This is not a matter of expressing hoped-
for initiatives or individual preferences that each
person, according to his or her specific role and
responsibility within the Church, always has the
right to hold and evaluate, but rather the very
foundations of faith, morals, and Catholic disci-
pline which the college of bishops together with
the pope have the mission of upholding. Finally,
there is a third paradox: the pope is being challenged just at the moment when there is a greater
awareness among other Christian confessions of
the urgent need for unity. I will never forget how
one of them, holding significant authority in his
respective community, confided in me after a
long conversation: "There is a need," he said,
"for unity to come about. Regardless of the
obstacles that continue to pile up, there are many
signs that the time is right. It is now clear that
unity cannot be achieved except with reference
to the bishop of Rome. Some adjustments will
have to be made to ensure that the various
traditions which have developed since the time
of separation are respected, but we are no longer
talking about the impossible." Except, he added,

and at this point his voice had a hint of concerned sadness, "we have to take into account that today the pope is being contested from within the Catholic Church itself. This is an enormous obstacle that risks slowing down the process toward unity."

My friend was not kidding. If the person of the pope is so contested today, often, in reality—if I can put it this way—it is because of what is most incontestable in him. By its very nature—indeed, this stands at the core of the papacy—the very function of Peter is vulnerable to being challenged. To be challenged is to do the greatest homage to the Petrine ministry. Everyone senses this and has a premonition of it to the point that the purpose of the Petrine ministry is guaranteed, no matter what opposition it encounters throughout history; that the light of Christian revelation dwells intact and that which for good reason is called the Christian revolution retains its inexhaustible force. It is the rock against which is dashed any attempt to pervert, destroy, or "radically change," as is clear from many critical moments in history. In the choir of the Church of Santa Maria dell'Anima, in the heart of papal Rome, one can read, on the tomb of Hadrian VI, an epitaph of melancholic beauty that I have often meditated on. It invokes the situation of the Church at the beginning of the sixteenth century and the renewal that would have taken place under this pope if he had not died too soon and if so many opposing forces did not stymie his attempts at reform. The Lord put Paul VI to the test no less than his predecessors; He was no easier on him. In return, unlike Hadrian VI, the Lord gave him time (and we hope that more time will be given him still) to go forward, in the face of every storm and countercurrent, to complete the program he had announced in the encyclical *Ecclesiam Suam* and the inaugural speech he gave at the twelfth session of the Council. One day, when an honest historian will take it upon himself to show the real life of the Church in the last fifteen years, then, once all the vain agitations have faded away, it will be clear without a doubt that the entire Christian push for fidelity under the impulse of Paul VI was aimed at nothing other than laying the groundwork so that the salvific action of the Church of Christ could move forward in the midst of a deeply changed world.

2

A Life for the Church

ANY BIOGRAPHIES OF Paul VI have been published. His life has been dissected from many different angles, and the years of his pontificate have been subject to particularly close scrutiny. There is no lack of interpretations, and only a comparison of their complementarity and differences would lead to a unified vision of what kind of a man Paul VI really was. What is more important for our purposes is the attempt to ascertain the heroic virtues he lived and his fidelity to following the Gospel. It will be important, then, to capture the unifying elements of his existence. The picture that emerges is a profound spirituality, tied to a consistent witness, evident in the various ministries he was called to perform. Such a life of faith cannot be improvised. Rather, it requires a long and patient preparation so that it will become efficacious and fruitful. His life was one conceived as abandonment to the mystery of grace to let God shape his existence to the point of making him an instrument of love extended to everyone without exclusion.

His years in Brescia

Giovanni Battista Montini became a child of God through Baptism in the parish church of Concesio on

September 30th, 1897. Through a mysterious twist of providence, a young religious sister in Lisieux, having reached a profound state of holiness within a short period of time, was preparing to enter her heavenly homeland that same day: Thérèse of the Child Jesus. At the baptismal font, the parents, Giorgio and Giuditta Alghisi, gave their second born the names Giovanni Battista, Enrico, Antonio, and Maria. He was born on September 26th in the family home. Suffering from weak health, Battistino, as he was affectionately called, was looked after lovingly by his nurse, Clorinda Zanotti. The future Pope would always place great confidence in her, especially when passing long periods of time with his playmates. Mamma Giuditta often took the child to areas with healthier air so he could breathe more easily. Giovanni Battista grew up within the school of a healthy, hard-working family of believers together with brothers Ludovico and Francesco. During a visit to Concesio some years ago, I was able to touch with my own hands one of the first pieces of Giovanni Battista's writings. It consisted of birthday greetings to his father. The child's handwriting reveals the lovable soul behind it. The text expresses a promise that he will always be obedient and good. It was in fact a promise he kept by a lifestyle centered on a few, essential elements that took root in the heart of little Montini. He received First Holy Communion on June 6th, 1907, and Confirmation on June 21st. These moments left a deep impression on his mind as important steps on his journey to a complete gift of self to the Lord.

Giovanni Battista continued to grow and mature. He persevered at school despite health problems that prevented him from attending classes regularly. Regardless, he received excellent marks. In his teen years, he frequented the Oratorio della Pace run by the *Filippini* Fathers. At that time, the Oratory was a privileged place for Christian and cultural formation. It was here that he met Fathers Paolo Caresana and Giulio Bevilacqua, who remained close friends throughout his entire life. Father Paolo had a particularly important role in Giovanni Battista's priestly discernment. This clearly emerges from a letter dated September 11th, 1913:

> I think it's a good thing for you to take this opportunity to speak openly to R. P. Caresana about your plans for the future. His advice could be very useful to you at this time, and in matters of such great importance it never hurts to listen to the advice of level-headed and holy people. In any case, I leave it to you to judge how best to keep yourself balanced. May the Lord inspire you, watch over you, and bless you.

In effect, Giovanni Battista went forward allowing the decision to pursue the priesthood mature gradually in his heart. He made this very clear later when speaking as Pope to a group of Benedictines: "I was in a sort of ecstasy; without doubt, it was there that God implanted in my soul the first stirrings of a desire to consecrate myself to his service." In any case, it was in 1915 that he became fully conscious of his choice to dedicate himself to the Lord and acted upon it. He went with Father Caresana and Father Galloni to the Camaldolese hermitage of San Genesio. At that time, the rule of the hermitage prohibited priests from receiving lay guests while lodged within the cloister. After some insisting by the two priests, Giovanni Battista was allowed to stay in a storage room of the woodshed out back. "It's not terribly cold right now, so with a few good blankets you should be able to sleep well enough." With these few laconic words, Father Matteo, Master of the Hermitage, allowed him to stay a week with them. Father Galloni writes:

> In August of 1915, Giambattista said to me, "let's go to Mount San Genesio since I'd like to take a few days retreat myself." "Certainly," I replied. It seemed to me that Giambattista had to make some pretty big decisions. We got ourselves organized within a couple of days and went. Father Caresana, who was my confessor at the time, came with us. We arrived at the place after a long and exhausting trip. Public transportation was not like it is today. We knocked on the door of the hermitage. Father Matteo, whom I knew well, came and opened for us. I asked if they had room for us to make a retreat. "For you two priests, sure," he said. "But not for that young lad there. The rule prohibits us from letting laymen in." "But Father Matteo," I pleaded, "we've travelled two hundred kilometers to come here. We can't stay and send the lad back. Please, make an exception to the rule." Father Matteo took the matter to the Father Superior. The response was the same: a layman cannot enter the hermitage. "If the kid wants to stay," he reasoned, "he'll have to sleep out back in the woodshed. We can throw a mattress on the floor." "Thanks, Father," Giambattista said beaming. For that entire time—we were up there for about a week—Giambattista Montini, who was used to living in a noble house and who was suffering from delicate health, slept on a mattress on the floor of a woodshed. Perhaps it was during that week of solitude, during a prayerful retreat at

> a hermitage, that he decided to follow the voice
> of God calling him to the priesthood.

That's exactly how it happened. The young Montini not only accepted with enthusiasm the need to sleep on the floor of a woodshed, but throughout the week, in prayerful solitude, he began to understand clearly what his future would entail. "I will spend my life fixed on heavenly things." That is how he summarized those days of retreat in a letter written to his good friend Andrea Trebeschi, to whom he confided his decision to enter the seminary. "And this is why such news should come as no surprise to you, my friend, who know me so well. So here it is: I am starting to take classes at the seminary today."

The day was October 20th, 1916. He had decided to enter the seminary. His life would be dedicated to the service of God. A letter of his mother Giuditta also attests to this. Sharing the news with her sister-in-law Elisabetta, she describes her son's feelings in setting out on this new path:

> It seems quite clear to me that our dear son is
> entering the halls of the seminary in a spirit of
> humility, goodwill, abandonment to God, and
> with a great love for Him. We are therefore
> confident about this development in his life.
> May the light toward which our lives are
> directed inspire and enliven us so that we don't
> give up or lose our way along the journey.

Montini's fickle health did not allow him to board at the seminary so he enrolled as a commuter student. This, however, in no way hindered his spiritual and cultural formation. He carried out his pastoral formation at various institutions, and above all, at the Oratory of Saint Philip Neri. He was also directly involved with *Fionda,* a cultural association founded by his friend Trebeschi. The years passed and Montini was finally ready to receive sacred orders: first the diaconate, then the priesthood. He was ordained on March 8th, 1920. The chasuble in which he celebrated his first Mass was woven from the wedding dress of his mother Giuditta. Montini was calm, but he knew his life was about to change dramatically and would require him to give himself completely to the Lord. This is clear from letters he wrote to relatives and his closest friends. He began his priestly service at a parish where he was admired not only for his humility and simplicity, and also for his deep Eucharistic devotion.

Years in Rome

The time arrived for more intense service. The Bishop of Brescia, Monsignor Gaggia, sent Montini to the Lombard College in Rome to complete his studies. Here he dedicated himself to the study of philosophy at the Gregorian University and to literature at the Sapienza. Visits from his father, a Deputy in the Italian Parliament, and from his brother Ludovico made this time away from family and pastoral duties a bit more tolerable. And in any case, new roads were opening for Father Montini. He was summoned by the then-Substitute of the Secretariat of State, Msgr Pizzardo, who asked him to prepare himself to enter the *Pontificia Accademia dei Nobili,* the prestigious training ground for Vatican diplomats. Fr Montini was not very enthusiastic about the request. This is evident in a letter written by his Bishop to the Substitute of the Secretariat of State asking for a *nihil obstat*:

> Father Montini, about whom Your Excellency
> has asked me, has all the best qualities one

could desire in a priest: a rare mind, a heart of gold, an iron-strong will, a love for study, and above all such piety that everyone who knows him cannot help but love and admire him. His fellow students looked upon him as an authority figure and accepted whatever advice he had to give as if it were a command. This is the reason I regret having him taken away from my diocese, now in need of so many priests like him; indeed, I was already thinking he would be the perfect chaplain for young people for whom he would have done so much good. But he lacks only one thing: good health. Here in Brescia, he would have been under the care of a tender and loving mother and therefore able to sustain his work load and not lose the little health he had, since he is also suffering in his heart. I don't mean to oppose your intentions by saying that, for I would regret giving you a "no" answer, even if I could do so in good conscience, because I know how much he is needed and wanted at the Vatican. But I have to say that if Fr Montini gives in and says "yes," it would be because of his good virtue and not because he would like an office life or the life of a diplomat. By his own volition, he would have liked to have had a care for souls; or rather—as I have always thought—he would have made a good Benedictine monk because of his studiousness and piety. He would have embraced the care of souls to do good and perhaps because it would have let him attend to his studies, among which, I believe, he liked "cold" Canon Law the least...

On November 20th, 1921, Fr Montini walked through the doors of Piazza della Minerva, 74. The first thing he wanted to do was to write home and open his heart about this new experience as a priest:

> My dearest loved ones, I've spent the entire day at the *Accademia* where I've dedicated this rainy Sunday to putting my things in order so that, I hope, I can begin an ordered life. I still don't know what to think about starting here, what to make of the environment and the studies. It seems to me there is room for a certain independence and the possibility to have some solitude. That consoles me a bit, because solitude allows one to build up the energy to be in company with others. I'm thinking of the day two years ago, which already seems far away but conjures up the same sentiments. I have the vague feeling I've fallen headlong into this and don't know which way is up; and I almost feel the need to stumble again in order to land back on my feet. But I am also experiencing divine help which in the past has helped me when I was "turning around and around," so that, provided it's not shock, I feel at peace. Besides, the Lord cannot but hear our prayers, and yours are especially strong right now because of the distance from the situation—indeed, that actually makes you closer—and because of the piety that inspires them.

Montini adjusted quickly. His enduring concern was to "interpret the Gospel into this language": that is, the language of diplomacy which was foreign to him at that time. The following summer Montini travelled to Austria and Germany to study German. Here he made a new friend, Mariano Rampolla del Tindaro, with whom he would form a close relationship in the years to come. In December of that year he received his degree in Canon Law from the Seminary in Milan. The academic portion of his preparation for direct service to the diplomatic corps was now complete. What now emerged, however, was uncertainty about where he would perform that service. In another letter to his family, he pours his heart out: "I'm enjoying the wait, but the uncertainty does make me a little nervous. I don't know yet how I should use my time." A few months passed before Montini received his assignment. He was told his first destination would be the Nunciature in Warsaw. The assignment called for all his energy and concentration. The fifty letters he wrote home bear those sentiments: the uncertainty of a ministry he was not entirely enthusiastic about, but a complete trust and abandonment to the Lord's will.

After about a year, Montini left Warsaw to begin work in the Vatican Secretariat of State in Rome where, among other things, he became Chaplain to the Roman branch of the Catholic Youth movement (*Gioventù Cattolica*), which was a prelude to his nomination as Chaplain of *FUCI* (the Italian Catholic University Federation). He spent summers in France. The cultural heritage of that country held a particular fascination for Montini. Its artistic beauty and intellectual freshness would have a deep effect on him for the rest of his life. When he returned to Rome, Father Agostino Gemelli proposed that he go to Milan and work with young people at the Catholic University there. Msgr Pizzzardo got to him first, however, and enlisted him to work as a *minutante* in the Secretariat of State. From the 1931–1932 academic year until 1937, Montini also taught a course in the history of Pontifical diplomacy at the *Utriusque iuris* Institute at *Apollinare*. These years in Rome were also marked by a deep spirituality. Living proof of this can be seen in the notes Giovanni

Battista took during a week of spiritual exercises at
Montecassino with Father Bevilacqua:

> To choose the humblest duties in the Church
> insofar as they promote the Reign of God. To
> have no ambition for a career. To prefer to be
> an apostle rather than a jurist. A pastor instead
> of a canon or religious. A missionary rather than
> a functionary. A teacher rather than a scholar.
> One needs to have a realist mindset in the
> Church and not the usual, ambitious mindset
> when it comes to assigning tasks: to be fearful
> rather than desirous of advancement and to
> prefer positions where one must exercise
> greater virtue and self-denial. *Ecce ancilla
> Domini.* This is the reason for authority in the
> Church. Not so that it may be fostered in itself,
> much less appropriated for oneself. When one
> receives an office in the Church, it is necessary
> that: (1) it be exercised with determination and
> courage. Not to get down on oneself or get
> discouraged or to narrow the possibilities;
> rather to strive, risk, and dare with prudence
> and faith to make that office as fruitful as
> possible. Any desertion of the office—from
> second guessing, laziness, or exhaustion—is,
> except in reasonable cases, against the Holy
> Spirit given in the diaconate. One therefore also
> needs to lead by command. One must also
> tolerate infelicitous outcomes of one's labor. (2)
> One must also pay attention to the real needs
> of souls and how to meet them where they are.

Special mention must be made of Montini's work as
chaplain of *FUCI* insofar as it played a key role in
inflaming his pastoral zeal and honing his theological
readiness. Father Giovanni Battista urged the members
of *FUCI* (the *fucini*) to balance their studies at the

university with a careful study of Christian teaching. To this end, he prepared outlines of various lessons that showcase his academic strengths. One finds in these pages citations of such authors who nourished his mind such as Newman, Lagrange, Grandmaison, Sertillanges, Marmion, and Prat. In short, a new line of theology that did not undermine the need for a Thomistic philosophical formation, but, fortified by such a formation, went on to explore new ways of understanding the faith. Step by step, the young Montini was opening his mind to a broad range of thinking that would remain his theological foundation for years to come. Yet it would be a mistake to think his efforts were only intellectual. He was able to instill in the *fucini* a newfound appreciation for the beauty and depth of the liturgy as an experience of the Church and as a sacramental reality allowing one to live in communion with the Church. Nello Vian, who would go on to become a distinguished editor of *L'Osservatore Romano*, gives a beautiful testimony to those years and how Don Montini displayed an extraordinary ability to understand young people.

> I first heard Msgr Giovanni Battista Montini speaking about Jesus Christ toward the beginning of '31 at a meeting of the Catholic University Circle in Rome at Piazza Sant'Agostino 20. He was seated at the end of a long table, giving a lesson on a topic which he subsequently published the same year in a dense book entitled *The Life of Christ* (followed, in 1934, by *An Introduction to the Study of Christ*). His voice was firm with a steely edge, and he would raise it significantly, almost jarringly, whenever emphasizing an important point. For me it was a sign of an interior fire that he

breathed through his speech. It struck me as full of spiritual energy that contrasted with his weak physical appearance. I began to attend *FUCI* regularly... On August 4th, 1932, I set out from France to the United States to take some courses in library science at the University of Michigan in Ann Arbor. When I got there, feeling lonely and being so far away, I decided to write to Msgr Montini to seek some spiritual advice. He responded right away with a multi-paged letter dated September 25th written from the Vatican. He is how it began: "Dear Vian, I received your (*tua*) letter [translator's note: the informal mode of address in Italian] and I performed a sort of examination of conscience to understand why in the world you would offer me your confidence and trust. I was overtaken by a moment of consternation and fear that I would feel so close and fraternal to a soul so far superior to mine and, more than an object of affection, an object of true esteem. But then I immediately remembered how fortunate we are as priests to have such relationships and how they are a gift from the Lord, for which we render thanks and enjoy them." I don't have to add anything to the tone, the generosity, and the height of virtue contained in that letter, addressed to someone he had just recently met.

These are the years when Montini began to fashion his priesthood on a pattern of true sanctity. It's enough to read a few notes he jotted down as a sketch of a "rule of life" to understand his journey toward a rock-solid personality.

I have to love silence, concentration, method-ology, and a schedule if my studies are to bear any fruit or virtue. I cannot waste my time and

> energy in frivolous reading but must search for what is good... I will make a concerted effort to keep my mind free of useless doubts and pessimism, impure fantasies and devious, duplicitous, and egocentric intentions, from laziness in research and reflection... I will cultivate within me a passion of fidelity to the Church as the Teacher of truth...

Life, however, never proceeds perfectly according to one's plans. Montini's dedicated ministry to *FUCI* was not looked upon benevolently by everyone, and especially the Jesuits in Rome, who thought they had sole responsibility for the organization. And they were not the only ones. Other voices of objection were raised. Suspicions arose from the fact that Giovanni Battista was the son of the Honorable Giorgio Montini, a Deputy in the Italian Parliament and politically active in the country, but not at all prone to allowing himself to be courted by Fascism and its thirst for power. So it happened that forces began to work behind the scenes to alienate Giovanni Battista. Among his most fierce critics was Msgr Luigi Ronca, a promoter of the "Roman party" who opposed Montini because of his political leanings. His nomination caused not a few problems within the Circle. The only solution Monsignor Ronca could come up with was to denounce Don Giovanni Battista to the Cardinal Vicar, Marchetti Salvaggiani, who in turn referred the complaint to the Substitute, Msgr Pizzardo. Montini was summoned to respond to the criticisms against him. His responses sufficiently disproved the truth of the accusations. What Msgr Ronca had actually accused Montini of was inculcating young people with the idea that faith should be rationalized at the expense of traditional devotions and practices. What Montini was actually

proposing was a study of the faith and prayers
expressed in the Psalms so as to make faith and prayer
virtually interchangeable. The *lex credendi* and *lex
orandi* were closely tied to give solidity to the testimony
of the *"fucini"*. In any case, to Msgr Ronca and others,
this seemed excessively innovative given the general
culture of the time and sounded like a betrayal of the
faith itself. Don Montini did not believe the accusations
were fair. Nevertheless, *pro bono pacis*, his superiors
deemed it best for him to cease his activity with *FUCI*.
For his part, Montini felt obliged to withdraw, and this
was the cause of no little consternation among the
young people who, unsurprisingly, could not understand the reason for the humiliation of Msgr Montini.
Amid all this strife, however, Don Giovanni Battista
showed a profound sense of reverence for the Church
and obedience toward his superiors, as evidenced by
letters to his family and his bishop at the time. A letter
to his family dated May 15th, 1932, reveals the state of
his soul:

> The entire spiritual and cultural dimension of
> my work has been affected by this; first by a
> series of strange notes that, even after I made
> some sense of them, did not amount to very
> much; then by advice which, in practice, would
> have weakened the effectiveness of whatever
> meager good I thought I was doing. I found
> myself in a position of defending myself against
> things that were at the same time both serious
> and ridiculous. But in the end I decided to
> accept this trial as something the Lord had
> given me. It didn't reach the point where I had
> lost the confidence of my superiors. But it did
> reach the point where the wind was taken out
> of the sails of our movement, which in recent

gatherings seemed to have gained momentum and to have reignited other people and other organizations.

A detailed "report" of the matter can be found in a long letter, dated March 19th 1933, sent by Father Montini to his Bishop in Brescia, Msgr Gaggia. It is worth considering this letter at length since it is important for understanding the dynamic of what happened and the state of Montini's soul:

> Your Excellency, I believe it is my filial duty to inform Your Excellency of the reasons for which I resigned from the chaplaincy (translator's note: Montini's official title was *Assistente Ecclesiastico Generale*) of the University Associations of Catholic Action. The reasons for my abrupt and untimely resignation after having been recently reconfirmed in the position and at the busiest time of the academic year are not limited to the responsibilities of my other job at the Secretariat of State. It is true that this position was becoming less compatible with my primary duties and that I was finding less time to devote to them as a result. There were times I even thought of asking you to dispense me from my duties at the Secretariat if the good of the students demanded that it would have been better for me to dedicate myself exclusively to serving them. But the fact is that my resignation was provoked by a certain opposition which I still don't fully understand. I can only attribute it to the will of God who permitted it to happen. The opposition began sometime last year. It seems to me that it is based on the desire of some Jesuit Father to take the university movement into his own hands and that our own movement was intimidating similar move-

ments under the Jesuits' care. I always aimed at
mutual understanding and maintained cour-
teous, friendly, and professional relationships
with everyone involved. But the Jesuit Fathers
are at a moment of panic and are wielding their
power: panic because they don't believe they
are surrounded by people of goodwill and thus
are prone to suspecting some plot against them,
and power because they work hard and enjoy
a high reputation within the Roman Curia. For
these reasons some were making me out to be
an anti-Jesuit and therefore as someone whose
every attitude, be it practical or doctrinal,
needed to be carefully watched and thus as
someone to whom there was no reason not to
attribute malicious intentions. These insinua-
tions were enough to have the Cardinal lose
faith in me, who up to that time had been so
generous toward me that it bordered on parti-
ality: he was extraordinarily favorable toward
the Jesuit Fathers and he couldn't tolerate
anyone being less so. His Eminence made a
remark to this effect. You can guess what would
have happened if I was not extremely cautious
after this, but it didn't matter. In any case, it is
good that Your Excellency know something
about the source of my troubles; nothing, absolutely nothing seemed to happen that should
have given offence to the Jesuit Fathers. I never
stole a single young person away from their
activities; to the contrary, I tried to encourage
our young people to attend them. I never tried
to lord it over them with the initiatives of
Catholic Action; in fact, I always showed understanding and kindness toward the Jesuit Fathers
in order to accommodate their young people
into Catholic Action without undermining their

autonomy or the soundness of their instruction. I only had to defend, in turn, the autonomy of Catholic Action and its impartiality toward undertakings similar to its own. It wasn't easy making others understand this right; a right equal to that which was peacefully enjoyed by those accusing us of being competitive. In some cases (e.g., regarding the associated "participants", the activity of the Missions, the religion courses, etc.), the Holy Father himself had to be consulted so that there would be no confusion about what he really wanted. The Pope repeatedly said we were right. I can provide documentation. But the truce was only apparent and brief. In April or May of last year, I began to feel I was surrounded by an air of suspicion and scorn. The very sympathy our young people had for our work was damaging to me. Also damaging was a religion course which, after the Ecclesiastical Assistant of the Roman Association had been begged three times to offer it, was entirely the creation of the Jesuit Fathers, and which I myself offered to the Association: the claim was that it was an alternative to the courses at the Gregorian University even though there was no scheduling conflict and it was offered before the Institute for Cultural Religion for the Laity was inaugurated. I subsequently asked my superior, His Excellency Monsignor Pizzardo, the reason for all this suspicion. He shared with me a number of observations about my work as Ecclesiastical Assistant that still leave me stunned. Some were downright false, others inconsistent. Monsignor Pizzardo himself never tired of assuring me of this since he knew the storm had subsided after he had told His Holi-

ness my side of the story. He told me to pay no
more attention to the complaints and to apply
myself all the more vigorously to the apostolate;
not to worry about all the grumblings which, if
they had had even an ounce of truth, he would
have told me to halt my activity. These observations always sprung from the same source;
but the one who brought them to the attention
of my superiors was the Cardinal Vicar, and he
did so with the stubbornness he was known for.
When I learned this, I tried to explain myself to
His Eminence, but his mind was already set and
it would have been useless to bring forward the
facts and refute the accusations point by point.
He wasn't going to budge on his opposition to
my work and my commitment to the movement. Indeed, his opposition was not based
merely on little, misleading pieces of information he was receiving, but rather on a stronger
opposition to Catholic Action in general which
he was not afraid to share openly, especially for
its central direction and means of operation,
which he showed genuine disdain for and
wished to eradicate completely or at least
render completely ineffective. Yet in practice he
defended and strongly supported Catholic
Action in Rome. From that moment I
completely abstained from any activity or ties
with the Roman Association, in which there
were many young people strongly attached to
me who were hurt by my absence but no less
willing to follow obediently, with my encour-
agement, other leaders and other directives.
And in this way I thought I had smoothed out
any friction until two things happened almost
simultaneously which revealed the Cardinal
Vicar's disdain for me. The first of these was a

survey that went out to all our Ecclesiastical Assistants eliciting suggestions on how to prepare the students (especially our students) for Easter. The wording of these suggestions had not changed in three years and was warmly welcomed by the universities because of the successful results theretofore. I've attached a sample of the survey here. These surveys passed from my hands to other unknown hands, and from there were passed onto the Cardinal Vicar together with serious accusations of "liturgism" and "Protestant" methods offensive to Catholic piety and particularly to the recitation of the rosary, etc. To these the Cardinal Vicar added an accusation of his own about the usurpation of tasks reserved to the Bishop. This was the heart of the problem. His Eminence did not know that the suggestions were nothing more than that: suggestions, not orders or directives, but rather "observations" simply "to offer direction" and based on the experience of previous years to ensure that the initiative would be a success. His Eminence had no idea that the religious scope of these observations was intended primarily for people far from religion, skeptical and even hostile to the normal forms of worship. He hadn't even considered the fact that these instructions, whatever they might be, had no practical effect on the city of Rome since the Easter celebrations for University students were prepared by the University Chapter. And finally, he hadn't noticed that these "suggestions" were based directly on initiatives the Cardinal Vicar himself had wisely and enthusiastically promoted in Roman parishes as reflective of true Catholic tradition and authentic Christian sensibility.

The other factor that worked against me were complaints within the Catholic University Association of Rome of overly authoritative attitudes and an insufficient understanding of young people allegedly attributable to methods supported by the Cardinal Vicar. I had no part at all to play in this spat, directly or indirectly. I was completely detached from it. Nevertheless, someone suggested to the Cardinal Vicar that this internal strife was entirely attributable to the University Federation and to me in particular, as if we were the instigators or at least the protectors of the instigators, or as if we had excused them from being obedient to ecclesiastical authorities. "As soon as they go to the Federation," it was said (though, for the record, only a few were coming to us and only those with specific jobs), "they come away poisoned." It should be noted that these dissidents were the cream of the crop as far as attitude, loyalty, and devotion: everybody knows them. The Cardinal Vicar, with frightening disdain, reported me to my Superior, His Eminence the Cardinal Secretary of State, and to His Excellency Msgr Pizzardo. The latter showed that he was clearly shaken by these accusations: he took it upon himself to shed some light on the facts and to defend an unjustly accused member of the Secretariat of State. But he clearly did not want to naysay the Cardinal Vicar. He seemed to be conflicted, torn, and hesitant. I made it clear to him that if I wasn't defended, at least with regard to the actual circumstances and facts of the case, I would no longer be able to work effectively and peacefully. He showed signs of disappointment, but nevertheless he resigned himself to the possibility that I would have to leave my work. The fact is that after an animated discussion with him (at which Righetti was also present), in which I understood clearly that he was not inclined to take action and defend the truth about Catholic Action and about me, I presented him my resignation. This took place on February 13th. He then bade me call His Eminence Cardinal Pacelli (not in regard to my resignation, but in regard to the accusations of the Cardinal Vicar), and with great generosity he took up the charges against me with His Eminence the Cardinal Vicar. He also was not accurately informed about the Easter mailing and the facts about the Roman Association. He shared a few observations with me. It wasn't hard to offer him an explanation which in the end seemed to satisfy him. In addition to commending, with paternal affection, my work at the Secretariat of State, he didn't hide from me his wonder that I would take upon myself such a decision for reasons external to the office: I had to tell him humbly that for the last ten years I had been serving as spiritual director to the students not through my own volition, but by the order of His Excellency Monsignor Pizzardo; an order repeatedly reaffirmed by the Holy Father. In other words, I understood that he would have happily seen me leave my involvement with Catholic Action. So I went to see His Eminence the Cardinal Vicar, together with Msgr Coffano (who had also signed the incriminating circular letter, but was, in fact, innocent of any wrongdoing). I tried to respond calmly and with utmost sincerity to each accusation I deemed unjust. He remained steadfast in his overall negative judgment toward Cath-

olic Action, even if he was unable to support
that negative judgment in regard to the usual
grievances he had against the central steering
committee of Catholic Action. There had been,
in fact, by our own request, an investigation into
every aspect of the Roman Association that
could have raised suspicion. This was actually
quite distressing to the young people who knew
well the truth of the matter. The investigation
was carried out with such distrust and such a
desire to find us guilty that there were some
young people, including a Professor at the
University, who declared themselves ready to
testify in our favor under solemn oath. Despite
the mean-spiritedness surrounding the investigation, it would nevertheless have shed light
on the truth of the situation if it had not been
cut short before it could even begin to restore
my reputation and that of my outstanding
collaborators. I wasn't even given a chance to
respond to questions. The thing dragged on for
some time. There was still some way to uncover
the damage His Excellency Pizzardo had done
with his unfounded campaign against our work
and my subsequent resignation. But the increasingly hostile and threatening attitude of His
Eminence the Cardinal Vicar had persuaded
His Excellency Pizzardo to offer my resignation
to the Holy Father and to obtain for me, based
on circumstantial needs and my duties at the
Secretariat of State, relief from my responsibilities associated with the chaplaincy at *FUCI*
effective February 22nd. The Holy Father, Msgr
Pizzardo told me, had kind words for me and
my work. At an audience Dr Righetti had with
the pope on the following day, His Holiness
reaffirmed his favorable judgment toward me

and read, with Dr Righetti present, the Easter
circular letter, making some amusing comments
about the grammar, but also remarking that he
had no objections to its doctrinal content. In a
subsequent audience with Dr Righetti, the Holy
Father again expressed his affection and
support for me and our work, making it abun-
dantly clear that circumstantial reasons, and not
anything I had done, prompted him to accept
my resignation letters, which I've enclosed with
this letter. I have to say in all honesty that from
the moment those letters were accepted by him
as definitive, he has had nothing but words of
support, esteem, and praise for me, even, if I'm
not mistaken, in the presence of the Cardinal
Vicar. Throughout this whole affair I've also
had the moral support of His Excellency Archbishop Ottaviani (Substitute of the Secretariat
of State and my direct Superior); even he
expressed it mostly behind closed doors. Even
he, who knows the whole affair and the people
involved, affirmed for me the need to step away
from my work with the young people. I should
also add that, even though I may not have
deserved or expected it, I have been blessed
with the fidelity of so many young people,
priests, and professionals from all over Italy,
something that had certainly not lessened the
regret I feel in leaving this work which has been
so dear to me and just at the time when it was
beginning to bear fruit so naturally.

As is clear from this letter, even a relatively marginal
affair such as the *FUCI* ordeal reveals the spiritual and
human maturation taking place in Martini and preparing him for more serious pastoral responsibilities. His
stepping down from the chaplaincy at *FUCI* did not

indicate a lessening of interest in the spiritual lives of
the young people attracted to him. So the young Father
Giovanni Battista, working full-time at the Secretariat
of State, forged ahead with giving spiritual direction
and preaching spiritual retreats whenever the opportunity arose. Looking at his notes for these spiritual
conferences, we see an impressive elaboration of the
Church's teaching that remains firmly within her
tradition while also reflecting a healthy theology that
would subsequently be "vindicated" a few years later
at Vatican II.

The Years at the Secretariat of State

The first major turning point in the priestly life of
Father Giovanni Battista occurred in 1937 when he was
entrusted with an enormous responsibility. He was
appointed Substitute of the Secretariat of State on
December 15th. The words of his predecessor in the
position, Msgr Tardini, best express the significance of
that day. This is what he wrote in a letter addressed to
the father of the new Substitute:

> He has been more than a friend but a brother to
> me during my time as Substitute. Having
> witnessed firsthand his talent, spirit of sacrifice,
> and extraordinary virtue, I couldn't help but be
> immensely pleased as his nomination to succeed
> me. Not only because I see that his abilities have
> been recognized and rewarded, but particularly
> because I am sure the work of Father Giovanni
> Battista in such a prominent position will be of
> enormous benefit for the Church.

In effect, the Church would be in need of such a highly
talented individual, especially because of the sad turn

of events that would affect public life so deeply: the authoritarian turn of Fascism and the efforts Pius XI would make to counter it, as well as the Second World War that would put Montini on the front lines, together with Pope Pius XII, who succeeded Pope Ratti on March 2nd, 1939.

It is widely known that there was a close collaboration between and Pius XII and Msgr Montini. Worth highlighting is the high esteem the Pope had for his Substitute. If we look closely at Pacelli's speeches, we can easily detect how heavily he relied on Msgr Montini's notes, even to the point of quoting directly from them at times. This is no surprise. On the one hand, it's normal for staff members to prepare material for their superiors who use them as they see fit. On the other hand, there was an unusually high affinity between Pius XII and Msgr Montini. From their extraordinarily refined cultural preparation to their intense spirituality, Pius XII and Msgr Montini shared an ardent love for the Church and a strong sense of responsibility in performing their respective roles for Her wellbeing. In any case, during the war Montini played a hidden but key role, especially in light of the abundant documentation and archival evidence emerging after the war. The depth of Pius XII's esteem for Montini is clear from multiple testimonies. Particularly poignant is that of the particular secretary of the Substitute, Msgr Clarizio:

> The Cardinal Secretary of State, Eugenio Pacelli, had enormous appreciation for him and opened himself to Montini completely. Once he became Pope Pius XII, he reconfirmed his position and placed even greater trust in him, more than he did in another other ecclesiastical figure … He

was always phoning him on his personal line. He wanted him to be available around the clock and not engaged in any other activities, even pastoral. He personally met with him at least once a day, usually toward 8:00 in the evening. He always emerged from that meeting with a load of assignments and tasks for the entire Curia. This increased his workload greatly, encompassing tasks beyond those normally preformed by the Substitute of the Secretariat of State. Many people expressed their satisfaction for the swiftness with which he discharged his duties. Obviously, there was some jealousy as well. This strict collaboration continued until Montini departed from Rome to take up another assignment.

Similar testimony is given by Cardinal Casaroli who, summoning up personal memories of Msgr Montini, writes:

I remember how the Secretary of State, Cardinal Pacelli, always said that Msgr Montini was a "thorough and efficient worker." As far as I can remember, Cardinal Pacelli and Msgr Montini had an excellent relationship. Cardinal Pacelli continued to hold the same esteem for the Servant of God after he was elected Pope, taking the name Pius XII.

And that of Msgr Mario Brini:

He was summoned every evening (even on Christmas and Easter) to an audience with Pope Pius XII which lasted from about 8:15 p.m. to 9:30 p.m. or longer. He always carried back to his office a considerable pile of reports to sort through. During these audiences with His Holiness, Msgr Montini *always remained standing.* He had occasion to tell me this, and he reconfirmed it during an audience I had with him after I had become Bishop (1962). He had invited me to sit, but I remained standing, protesting that he did the same thing when in the presence of Pius XII. So he said to me, "yes, it's true. I never sat in his presence. But sit down anyway, if for no other reason than to make yourself more comfortable." Not only that, but I have to say that Substitute Montini *never even sat down when he was on the phone with the pope* (which was frequently). I was present and had to hold the notebook in which he took notes. Pius XII always wanted to have him "at his beck and call," so much so that the Servant of God felt obligated to transfer his public Sunday Masses from Sant'Ivo (at the Sapienza University) to the Oratory within Vatican City, near Saint Anne's Church, and finally to suspend them altogether.

He had to handle numerous delicate issues on a daily basis. Pius XII and Montini, though they had slightly different personalities, always discussed the serious problems of the day together. Above all, once the war had ended, there was an urgent question of how to go about reconstruction. There was also the question of Italy's political life, which Montini followed very closely, leading him to create a tight network of friends and colleagues of the pope—De Gasperi *in primis*—and many other former *Fucini* members including Andreotti, Moro, Veronese, Fanfani, and others. And we must not forget the international arena that, above all, was overshadowed by communist domination in the USSR and the suffering of many Christian Churches in the Communist block.

The Years in Milan

Montini's years of service at the Secretariat of State went by quickly. On August 30th, 1954, Ildefonso Schuster, the Cardinal Archbishop of Milan, passed away, prompting Pope Pius XII to nominate his Substitute, Msgr Montini, to succeed him in that important Archdiocese. Truth be told, it was already toward the end of 1948 when rumors began circulating that Montini would become the next Bishop of a major Italian diocese, and more specifically Venice. Montini himself, in a letter to his friend Father Bevilacqua, denied the rumor as having no basis whatsoever. We'll return to this fact a little later and the role it played in his beatification. To clarify the situation once and for all, it is crucial to remember what Montini wrote in a letter to Fr De Luca: "I am sizing up the formidable responsibilities of my ministry and I still feel anxiety about my ability to meet them: about my inadequacies and my weakness. I so much need God to take me by the hand."

Montini undertook two main tasks as he began to lead the Church in Milan: fidelity and defense of the Ambrosian tradition, as well as its renewal so that it might confront more effectively the challenges of the modern world. It was a prime example of the "New Evangelization." He was fond of repeating, *"Non nova sed nove"* to indicate the path of renewal. Christ remains the same "yesterday, today, and tomorrow" (Heb 13:8). But cultural and social changes drive the Church to undertake a pastoral renewal. These were years of intense pastoral action during which Montini hardly stopped to take a breath, maintaining a strict regimen of prayer, appointments, meetings, parish visits, ministry to the suffering, preaching, and administering the sacraments, pastoral visits and pastoral letters during Lent, overseeing the life of seminarians and priests, especially when so many were leaving the active ministry and were reduced to poverty at that time, as well as his visits to the United States, Brazil, and Africa. In short, a life patterned after the heart of Christ and dedicated to serving his brothers and sisters in a uniquely complicated diocese immersed in modern development. At the time of Pius XII's death, the Archbishop of Milan was still not a Cardinal. The election to the papacy of Giuseppe Roncalli, the Patriarch of Venice, who took the name of John XXIII, reminded Montini of the many occasions he had to meet with Roncalli both in Venice and Milan, each of which was full of mutual respect and affection. On the very day John XXIII was elected, before he went down to the Basilica of Saint Peter to be inaugurated, he wanted to write to the Archbishop of Milan to tell him he had created him a Cardinal and that his name would be first on the list of new Cardinals. This happened on December 15th, 1958.

The Return to Rome

Montini's ministry in Milan came to an end on June 21st, 1963, when he was elected Supreme Pontiff and chose the name of the Apostle to the Gentiles: Paul. It now became his responsibility to continue the work of the Council and the mission of the Church in a time of dizzying change. Among his first words, those that indicated the path to follow, bear repeating: "What are you, Church? And what do you have to say for yourself?" He did everything possible to make his voice heard, but perhaps the world wasn't listening or hadn't understood it. It was a time marked by innova-

tion and progress in a post-conciliar Church: his trip
to the Holy Land and a meeting with Athenagoras
indicated a great awakening in the ecumenical movement; he also made trips to the United Nations, India,
Turkey, Colombia, Australia, the far East, Indonesia,
as well as the Philippines where he was injured in an
attempt on his life on November 27th, 1970. At the
Sunday Angelus address after his return to Rome, he
simply said, *"ho perdonato e ho dimenticato"* (I have
forgiven, and I have forgotten). From that day on he
never mentioned the incident again. In the years that
followed, his pastoral visits to parishes in Rome
alternated with visits to various Italian dioceses to
strengthen his brothers and sisters in the faith. In short,
it is to these intense years, full of activity, that historians primarily turn their attention when interpreting
his Pontificate. But these do not get to the core of the
life of sanctity of Paul VI. What must receive more
attention—now that the evidence for beatification has
been analyzed—is Montini's complete and sincere
dedication to the Church at a moment of great difficulty in the midst of rapid changes of the modern
world and the errant interpretations of the Second
Vatican Council. These caused him immense suffering
as evident from abundant testimony. But his faith and
obedience to the call were even greater, and this is
what makes his legacy worth remembering. His teaching, especially as contained in the encyclicals, reveals
a sharpness of long-term vision that today convinces
us of the extraordinary intelligence and clarity with
which he thought. Several sayings of Paul VI have
become famous aphorisms and have reappeared in
subsequent Magisterial documents: "The world suffers
from a lack of thought," "development is the new

name of peace," "experts in humanity," "today's world listens more closely to witnesses rather than to teachers," "Politics is the highest form of charity." Underlying each of these expressions is Paul VI's remarkable acumen and capacity to analyze situations. A passage from one of his Wednesday Audiences manifests the soul of Montini on the eve of the great controversies which would explode in the Church and civil society:

> Where is the Church that we love, the Church that we desire? Was the Church of yesterday perhaps better than the Church of today? And what will the Church of tomorrow be like? A sense of confusion seems to spread even among the most faithful sons and daughters of the Church, even among the most renowned and authoritative of scholars. There is a lot of talk about authenticity, but where can we find it if so many important things, even essential things, are placed into question? There is a lot of talk about unity, and a lot of people seek to find it on their own terms; about the apostolate, but where are the generous and true apostles when vocations are diminishing and the spirit of cohesion is weakening among the Catholic laity? There is a lot of talk about charity, but we live in an environment of criticism and bitterness.

There are plenty of similar texts dating from the same years. Most striking is Paul's analysis of the phenomenon that caused him the most suffering. It was not so much attacks from outside the Church that troubled him, but those that were perpetrated in a vitriolic and acerbic way by people who professed to be Christian and Catholic. Paul VI was nonetheless able to evaluate the opposition with sharp acumen. He tried to analyze and identify intelligently the appeals for positive and

necessary change in the Church. However, his sense
of realism also dictated to his conscience *how* these
changes were to be implemented. He was never short
of courageous words such as, "there is no need to close
one's eyes to the ideological and social reality now
surrounding us. Indeed, it would do us well to look at
it in the face with courageous serenity." In this he
really did show himself courageous. He looked everything in the face, good and evil, never taking his gaze
off either. He even had to face slander during those
tumultuous years, including insinuating rumors about
his sexuality. This cruel and unfounded gossip was
concocted by cynical, unscrupulous figures aimed at
political manipulation, quite common at the time.
Nevertheless, Paul VI's humility and *parrhesia* pre-
vailed in these difficult circumstances. His humility
manifested itself in several gestures of profound
significance. His decision to refrain from wearing the
tiara, for example, a gift from the Archdiocese of Milan
and now housed in the Basilica of the National Shrine
of the Immaculate Conception in Washington, D. C.,
signified his renunciation of temporal power and his
preferential option for the poor. Another indelible sign
of his humility is found in the ecumenical event of
December 14th, 1975, on the tenth anniversary of the
cancellation of the mutual excommunications of East
and West. At the conclusion of a Mass celebrated in
the Sistine Chapel in the presence of Meliton, Metro-
politan of Chalcedon, the official representative of the
Patriarch of Constantinople, Paul VI approached him,
knelt before him, and kissed his feet. The powerful
symbolism of this gesture is not to be underestimated.
It hangs, in fact, upon the significance of the Council
of Florence in 1443. At that time, there was a concerted

effort to bring about a reunion of Catholics and Orthodox, but it was in vain. The resounding symbol of failure was the Orthodox bishops' refusal to kiss the foot of the pope, which was the customary sign of reverence. Paul VI's genuflection and reverent kiss of Meliton's feet symbolized that true "primacy" must be given to charity, to the one who knows how to humble himself and to forgive, acknowledging the true value of his brother. There are many similar signs of Montini's characteristic humility, all the more exemplary since he was chosen as the successor of Peter.

Neither can we forget Paul VI's heroic efforts during the abduction of Aldo Moro and his execution by the Red Brigade. The affection he had for this one-time fellow "*fucino*" and his clear understanding of the gravity of his abduction put Paul VI on center-stage during those weeks. His letter "to the men of the Red Brigade" and the homily he delivered to Moro's funeral will forever be numbered as Pope Paul VI's most courageous contributions in one of the most sad and tragic periods of Italy's modern history. The testimony of Father Magee reveals some of the hitherto unknown details of those excruciating weeks:

> The Servant of God was deeply distressed when his good friend Aldo Moro was kidnapped and for the way in which he suffered. He did everything he could to intervene and to free the statesman, even to the point of writing a letter to the Red Brigade and asking them "on bended knee" to free the Honorable Aldo Moro. I can say that the Servant of God did this "in the supreme name of Christ," hoping the Red Brigade would come to its senses and let him go. The day that Aldo Moro's body was discovered—I remember hearing it on television—I

went to see the Servant of God in his personal
bedroom where he was accustomed to taking a
short afternoon nap. He was still seated on the
side of the bed. It was almost as if he were
expecting the bad news. When I entered the
bedroom, he looked straight at me and said, "so
it's all over?", and I said to him, "Yes, Your
Holiness, Aldo Moro is dead." He immediately
got on his knees and prayed fervently for the
repose of his soul. The homily he gave for Aldo
Moro's funeral at Saint John Lateran Basilica
clearly showed the extent of his spiritual
suffering and his moral dejection from the pain
of knowing his dear friend was dead. Let me
add one more detail: that evening, the Servant
of God, while at Saint John's Basilica, wanted
to proceed by foot from the sacristy to the
cathedra. It was a rather long walk down the
nave and he was experiencing extreme arthritis
at the time. Yet he wanted to walk the length of
the Basilica on foot even though it wasn't
possible for him because they placed him on the
sedia gestatoria. He was really suffering inside
for having to submit to be carried on the *sedia
gestatoria* at a ceremony of remembrance and
prayer for his good friend Aldo Moro. He never
liked being carried on the *sedia gestatoria* and I
know that, whenever he was on it, he put on
the chains he was used to wearing underneath
his clothing to remind him that Christ had
carried the cross to redeem the world. No one
knew how much he suffered physically and
spiritually whenever carried on the *sedia gestatoria,* because he was always smiling. During
the ceremony for Aldo Moro at Saint John
Lateran, he was suffering even more because
he did not plan on being carried about on the

sedia gestatoria, even if he had no other choice
due to his physical condition.

Paul VI was in fact slowly approaching death and was
already prepared and willing to face it in order to flee
to the one whom he loved and served so dearly. Within
a few days, the urinary tract infection and accompany-
ing fever were wrecking havoc on his body. The
testimonies of Monsignors Macchi and Magee, his two
private secretaries, meticulously detail the day Paul VI
died and his attitude toward death: an attitude of utter
abandonment in prayer. He wanted to recite the
Profession of Faith and gave particular emphasis to
the line regarding the Church, repeating it several
times. He received Holy Communion as Viaticum and,
when asked by his secretary whether he wanted to
receive the Anointing of the Sick, responded firmly,
saying, "yes, right away, right away." His last words
were the *Pater Noster,* which he said repeatedly as if
invoking someone he trusted completely, unconditon-
ally placing his life into His hands. Let us read the
personal testimony of Msgr Macchi, Paul VI's private
secretary from November 18th, 1954 until his death,
about the last days of Paul VI's life on earth:

> In the summer of 1978, before going out to
> Castelgandolfo, he wanted to go around and
> greet all the sick Cardinals living in Rome. I
> think he was particularly keen on meeting with
> certain Cardinals who, at some point in the past,
> had hurt him. I emphatically told him how hard
> it would be to carry out these visits because of
> his ill health, but he just said, "I don't care." I
> think he wanted to go and make these visits in
> the same spirit he wrote his memoirs: that is, to
> assure everyone that he had forgiven them …
> on Thursday morning, Paul VI had an audience

with the new President of the Republic of Italy,
the Honorable Sandro Pertini. Just before the
audience, the pope was running a hundred-
degree fever. After the audience, the Servant of
God came into my office and, with the joyful
smile of someone who had just passed an exam,
he told me the President had not noticed he was
sick. The fever was still high on Friday ... On
Saturday evening, after a visit and consultation
with some professors, we had dinner around
8:00 p.m. The Pope came to the table. With me
was Msgr Magee, the other secretary, who had
just returned from vacation. We watched the
evening news on the television. After dinner we
retired to the adjoining room to recite the
Rosary together. Normally, the Pope liked to
say the rosary while strolling up and down the
corridor. On those evenings, however, still
feeling feverish, he preferred to remain seated.
Once we had finished the rosary, the Servant of
God wanted to go to his office to do some work.
I remarked that it might not be such a good idea
given the nagging fever. He was already on the
mend so it might be better for him to lie down
a while. So the Pope went to recite Compline in
the chapel. He stayed a while to pray more, and
then I accompanied him to his bedroom. When
he had gotten into bed, I brought him, as was
customary, some reports sent to him by the
Secretariat of State. As we had often done in the
past when the Pope was not feeling well, I read
him the documents and he dictated his
responses, which I would write on letterhead
of the Secretariat of State. After we he
proceeded like this for about an hour, I asked
the pope what he would like to do, and he asked
me to read him a few pages from *Mon petit*

catechisme of Jean Guitton which had just
arrived. After I had read the chapter on Christ,
the Pope told me to stop. Then he added: "The
night is coming on!" I should add that on the
previous evening, that is, on the night between
Friday and Saturday, the Pope had trouble
breathing due to his asthma. I rushed into the
room and helped him move from the bed to the
coach. Since there was always an oxygen tank
nearby, I thought it opportune to make use of
it. Once he had taken some oxygen, he immediately felt better. I remember that, as he was
sitting on the coach, he said to me, "Do you
remember when we were in Monteviasco on
the night Pius XII died, listening to the radio
reports relaying the last words of the Pope?" I
said I remembered it well, but I added that I
didn't think the moment had arrived yet for him
to die. Then he went back to bed and fell asleep
… He essentially began a very difficult night,
rolling back and forth continuously. So I
approached the bed and put my hands in his to
help him. The Pope withdrew his hands from
mine and placed them on my head. He was very
agitated! Recognizing how serious it was, I said
to the Servant of God, "should we recite the
rosary?" He answered, "Yes, certainly". Indeed,
at that point he asked me to give him absolu-
tion. I began the rosary in the hope that, being
a repetitive mediation, it might help him to
relax. But this was not the case. He was continually agitated until Doctor Buzzonetti arrived
around 3:00 a.m. … The next morning I awoke
around 7:00 a.m. and went directly to the Pope's
bedroom. I remember that he looked like
someone who had fought a battle all night long.
He looked exhausted and completely ener-

vated. The biblical image of Jacob wrestling
with the angel came to my mind. Given the
situation, I convinced the Servant of God that
it was inconceivable that he could offer Mass
on his own in this state, and that he should
therefore put it off until the afternoon … I came
back to check on him at about 11:00 a.m. and I
noticed that the Pope's alarm clock was ten
minutes slow. So I said jokingly said to the
Servant of God, "your clock is a little slow." He
said, "Reset it, please." I said, "but you know
you have always prohibited me from touching
this alarm clock because it is particularly
fragile." Paul VI responded, "Don't make things
so difficult." So I hurried up to adjust the clock,
which indeed was a very peculiar timepiece. It
was a gift from his mother when the Servant of
God went to Poland, which from that time he
took with him everywhere, set to awake him at
6:00 a.m. So I started to adjust it, not noticing
that I had accidently set the alarm to 9:40 and
wound it up. Then I stayed with the Pope. We
prayed and I read to him a little. At 12:00 noon
he wanted to get up and say the Angelus in the
chapel. When he got up to pray, all of us noticed
that it exhausted him just to stand on his own
feet. He was wobbling. As soon as we had
finished the Angelus, he went back to bed … At
around 5:30 p.m., I went to tell the Pope that I
would celebrate Mass at 6:00 p.m. and would
happily bring him Holy Communion. Paul VI
accepted the offer willingly. I should note that
in the Apostolic Palace at Castelgandolfo the
Pope's bedroom is arranged in such a way that
he can take part in the Mass … I myself celebrated the Mass. Paul VI followed the Rite
wearing a stole. When it came time for

Communion, I went to him to offer him the Body of Christ. Paul VI bowed toward the Eucharist with an expression of intense desire, as if he were dehydrated and approaching a spring of water. I then had the impression that this Communion would be the Servant of God's Viaticum, even though that thought had not occurred to me up until then that this might be his last Mass. At the end of Mass, after giving him the blessing, I went to ask him if he wanted to be anointed with the Oil of the Sick. The Servant of God said, "Yes, right away!" I should mention that, every year, when Paul VI would go to Castelgandolfo, he always brought the Holy Oils by hand. I administered the Sacrament of Holy Anointing of the Sick. The Pope responded to all the questions in the Ritual. He held out his hands and head to receive the holy anointing. When we finished the Rite, the Servant of God greeted me and those present with his right hand and then sank into deep prayer, as if he were already headed for the life to come. At that very moment, I had the impression that the illness completely overtook him ... Then a series of prayers began — the Our Father, Hail Mary, Hail Holy Queen, Soul of Christ — but the prayer that took primary place was the Our Father. At a certain point, the Pope simply kept repeating the prayer taught to us by our Savior. The Our Father was the last prayer he kept whispering until the moment of his death. At 9:40 p.m., the very moment of his *transitus*, the alarm clock rang. Cardinal Villot said to me, "shut off the alarm clock." But I, knowing it was a complicated mechanism, let it keep ringing, saying it would turn off automatically in a moment. This alarm clock, which woke him up

every day at 6:00 a.m., welcomed him that
evening into a new life: eternal life. I have
always considered the sound of that alarm a
particular grace from the Lord.

Fr Magee's testimony is not much different:

It was the Feast of the Transfiguration, one of
the Servant of God's favorite days in the liturgical calendar. He didn't even open his eyes.
We did everything we could to help him. We
put an icepack on his head because he was
running a fever of 111 degrees. He was burning
like a furnace and not saying anything, not even
murmuring. He just kept rolling back and forth
in his bed, night and day, putting his feet down
as if he wanted to get up and then putting them
back in bed again. At a certain point—and this
is very interesting because it was reported in
the news but inaccurately—he opened his eyes
and said to Msgr Macchi, "What time is it?" It
was strange for him to ask this because it
wouldn't have made much difference in the
state he was in. The room was dark. The
windows were all shut to keep him out of the
sun and the room fresh. Msgr Macchi answered,
"11:00." The Pope then looked at the little alarm
clock he always kept on his nightstand and
remarked, "Oh, look! My little alarm clock is as
tired as I am!" It was fifteen minutes slow. That
was why he asked Msgr Macchi in the first
place. He hadn't wound it up that evening ...
We had told the Servant of God he wouldn't be
saying the Sunday Angelus as was his custom.
So instead he got up and we brought him into
the chapel, supporting him up because he
couldn't even sit straight on his own. He recited
the Angelus with us. He said, "On this great

day of the Transfiguration, I am saying the Angelus for all the faithful of the Church." After he had recited the *Angelus,* he went back to bed ... he then sunk into a deep sleep almost miraculously, because we had asked the Lord to allow him to sleep so that his fever might subside ... At that point I sat down next to the Servant of God while he slept. Five minutes later he woke up, and for the rest of that afternoon, from 2:00 to 6:00, until the time Msgr Macchi celebrated Mass, the Servant of God repeatedly tried to get out of bed and I kept putting him back. Once he even managed to get out of bed, so I sat him into a chair. Then he indicated that he wanted to go back to bed. The doctors explained that this was a sign of delirium caused by the fever that was "boiling" in his head. Between 4:00 and 4:35 he managed to get out of bed thirteen times. After the thirteenth time he was exhausted. I was sweating profusely and hoping that he also was sweating. The room was extremely warm, and I was exhausted, unable to put him back into bed. At a certain point I said, "Your Holiness," but he didn't even look at me. He had his eyes closed and didn't say a word. Standing beside the bed, I called out even louder, "Your Holiness." He looked at me and recognized me immediately and said, "Yes, my dear," and I said to him, "Your Holiness, what do you want?" I wanted to do for him whatever he wanted. And what did he answer? As with a smile, he said, "My dear, a little patience." These were his last words. When someone is about to die, when he is really at the end, if there is someone around to hold his hand, it is very important. I learned this while I was a missionary in Africa. When one is about to die, he stands before a great abyss and has the sensation he is about to fall into it. If someone is holding his hand, it means everything psychologically, spiritually. The hand is very important; all the other senses pass away, but the hand remains sensible, and one feels everything through it. That is why I continued to hold the hand of the Servant of God. I think this is also the right thing to do pastorally. On that evening, I held the hand of the Servant of God as we started Mass. I can say that he himself concelebrated. He recited the entire Mass, which was in Latin. I remember that toward the end of the Creed, at the line, *"Credo in unam, sanctam, apostolicam Ecclesiam,"* he almost broke my hand he was squeezing it so hard. He repeated those words twice at that point, belting out with whatever strength was left in him, *"apostolicam Ecclesiam."* Then he recited the entire Eucharistic Prayer perfectly. Right after the consecration, while I was still holding onto his hand, he had a heart attack. It was so strong—like an explosion inside—that he rose from the bed. If I hadn't been holding onto his hand he would have fallen out of bed. I felt that hand as it was losing its pulse… We knew then that we were almost at the end. I noticed then that his whole body began to tremble. So I went over to him and said, almost yelling, "Your Holiness, it is time for Communion. Msgr Macchi is bringing you Communion"… Msgr Macchi came, the Pope received Communion, and I offered him a sip of water because he was unable to swallow and might choke. But he was able to drink it. After Mass, the situation got worse. Msgr Macchi approached the Servant of

God and asked him, "Your Holiness, would you like to receive the Sacrament of the Sick?" "Yes, right away!" he answered. It was if he was in a hurry to receive the sacrament. I went out at that moment ... While I was gone, Msgr Macchi gave Extreme Unction to the Servant of God. When I came back, I could hear how short of breath he was, how deeply he was trying to take in air ... he was hardly able to breathe. But he was still calm. He was breathing very heavily and we started to pray. The Sisters were with us, Franco Ghezzi, Cardinal Villot, the doctors, Msgr Caprio, Msgr Macchi, and myself. I stayed there, holding his left hand. At a certain point, we could hear his voice, even though it was feeble. Msgr Macchi asked us to be quiet because he thought the Servant of God was trying to say something and he wanted to be sure we could hear his last words. And what was the Servant of God saying? *"Pater Noster, qui es in coelis."* Until the very end we heard the Servant of God saying, *"Pater Noster, qui es in coelis."* He had nothing else to add; he had said everything. This went on until 9:30 p.m. At 9:30 he stopped... These were just about the last moments. At that moment the Servant of God opened his eyes and began to look at us, starting with the doctor who was positioned next to me. We were all kneeling. He looked at each of us in turn. Someone was still standing and he raised his eyes to see who it was. His eyes finally turned to Cardinal Villot, who was to his right and uttering the last prayers. He looked at Cardinal Villot, who was standing, and then, raising his head into an upright position, said, "Thank you." With his right hand he made the Sign of the Cross and fell into a deep sleep.

> There was no more agony. I felt his pulse as it
> gradually faded. At 9:41 p.m., the doctor said,
> "the Pope has died." At that moment, in silence,
> behind Cardinal Villot, the alarm clock started
> to ring.

At 9:40 p.m. on August 6th, 1978, the Solemnity of the
Transfiguration, Paul VI could have said the same
words Peter said to his Lord, "It is good for us to be
here" (Matt 17:4). The sense of mourning that broke
out among the people, shocked since the sickness had
overtaken him so suddenly, showed how much he was
loved. The funeral took place on August 12th in the
square in front of Saint Peter's Basilica with an enormous crowd taking part. The commotion of so many
people attested to the gratitude and affection they had
for a Pope who had been so battered but nevertheless
knew how to accept the love and esteem of the people.
The simple wooden coffin placed on the ground, just
like he wanted it, stands as a testimony to the greatness
of a Pope so fecund with humility and generous in
love. A passage from his will serves as an apt conclusion to this biographical summary of Paul VI:

> I fix my eyes firmly on the mystery of death and
> what comes after it, with Christ as my lamp, for
> he alone shines in the darkness; and therefore I
> look at death with humble and serene trust. I
> see the truth of it, which for me has always been
> reflected by this present life, and I bless the
> Victor over death for scattering the darkness
> and revealing the light. Therefore, in the face of
> death, in the face of a total, definitive detach-
> ment from the present life, I feel a need to
> celebrate the gift, the fortune, the beauty, and
> the destiny of this fleeting existence: O Lord, I
> thank you that you have called me to life, and

even more that, making me a Christian, you have regenerated me and called me to the fullness of life... I feel that the Church surrounds me: O holy Church, one, Catholic, and Apostolic, receive in this my parting blessing, my supreme act of love ... and, even more importantly, as I take my leave of this world and face the judgment and mercy of God, I have so many things I want to say; so many. Concerning the state of the Church: that she may have listened to something that We said, which for your sake We spoke with such gravity and love. Concerning the Council: see that it is brought to a fruitful implementation, and see that all its teaching is heeded faithfully. Concerning Ecumenism: may the work of drawing close to our separated Brethren continue in a spirit of mutual understanding, patience, and great love, but without swerving from true Catholic doctrine. Concerning the world: do not think it will be of benefit to take on its way of thinking, habits, tastes, but rather study it, love it, and serve it.

3

THE LIFE OF SANCTITY

STUDY OF THE theological life of Pope Montini reveals a deep spirituality pervading every crevice of his existence. Various testimonies taken on his behalf unanimously affirm that Giovanni Battista Montini had a profound experience of faith, motivated by a certainty of hope enlightening his life on earth, always oriented toward a perception of the greatness of the mystery of the resurrection, and rooted in a charity evident in every aspect of his daily living. Virtues, however, are never born in a vacuum. They require continual exercise and daily training on the part of the one who wishes to be a disciple of the Lord. Paul VI began to acquire these virtues from his childhood. His life of prayer emerged as a distinctive habit growing ever stronger through Eucharistic Adoration, a form of prayer that completely enveloped him as if he were really contemplating Jesus Christ in front of him.

A few testimonies merit particular mention as they were given by people who knew Giovanni Battista from his youth and attest clearly to his predisposition to prayer. Take, for example, that of Father G. Martinelli: "Simple, recollected, composed, this young, pale lad would stay on his knees, eyes closed, just as any other devout member of the faithful, but with an elusive intensity that made me certain he was gifted with an extraordinary participation in the intimacy of Christ." In any case, he exercised these spiritual qualities every day heroically in ordinary circumstances, making sanctity his true vocation, which he pursued with constant faith.

The dedication of faith

Faith. This word, essentially encapsulating the whole of Christian life, indicates a desire to abandon oneself completely to God who reveals himself (cf. *Dei Verbum*, 5). It is a theme worth probing more deeply in light of Paul VI's teaching. There are many texts we can ponder, but let a synthesis suffice:

> Faith shows trust in intelligence: it respects it, needs it, and defends it. And for the very fact that it strives to study divine truth, it imposes an obligation of absolute honesty of thought, to strive after something that does not weaken it, but strengthens, both in the natural speculative order and in the supernatural order... Faith requires action; it is a dynamic principle of morality. Faith demands a need for action which blossoms in charity; that is, in application, moved by a love of God and neighbor ... faith gives meaning to life and things; it gives hope in wise and honest work; it gives strength to suffer and to love. Yes, faith serves a purpose, and what a purpose! Our salvation!

We also can turn to the Year of Faith celebrated in 1967–1968. Pope Montini instituted it to celebrate, above all, the anniversary of the deaths of the Apostles Peter and Paul. It was an auspicious occasion to allow the People of God to reflect on the beauty and necessity of faith during a time of great confusion in the Church. It was Benedict XVI himself who recalled this event in *Porta Fidei.*

He thought of it as a solemn moment for the whole Church to make "an authentic and sincere profession of the same faith"; moreover, he wanted this to be confirmed in a way that was "individual and collective, free and conscious, inward and outward, humble and frank." He thought that in this way the whole Church could reappropriate "exact knowledge of the faith, so as to reinvigorate it, purify it, confirm it, and confess it." The great upheavals of that year made even more evident the need for a celebration of this kind. It concluded with the *Credo of the People of God,* intended to show how much the essential content that for centuries has formed the heritage of all believers needs to be confirmed, understood and explored ever anew, so as to bear consistent witness in historical circumstances very different from those of the past. In some respects, my venerable predecessor saw this Year as a "consequence and a necessity of the postconciliar period," fully conscious of the grave difficulties of the time, especially with regard to the profession of the true faith and its correct interpretation. (*Porta Fidei,* 4–5).

From more than one witness, we know that Paul VI lived the Year of Faith with particular intensity. At a tumultuous time, he wanted to write *The Creed of the People of God,* which remains to this day a genuine expression of the authentic faith passed on by a successor of Peter. The Year of Faith was particularly demanding for the Holy Father, especially in his efforts to communicate the importance of the faith and its contents as the Church had accepted them, meditated upon them, and passed them from one generation to the next. This is confirmed by Msgr Macchi, a close confidant of the Pope, who said, "the significance of this event during the Pontificate of Paul VI is particularly manifest in the seriousness with which he dedicated himself to giving a catechesis on the faith throughout the entire year, especially during his General Audiences on Wednesdays."

The faith, as mentioned previously, was a form of nourishment he first received from his family. As an old friend, Giovanni Ungari, recounts, Giovanni Battista's family displayed "exemplary religiosity that distinguished it from the average family," and the young Montini was fully aware of the preciousness of the gift of faith given him by his family. It was because of his family's witness to the faith, including his aunts and uncles, that Montini continually developed it and discovered a vocation to the priesthood through it. In this context, it is worth remembering what the young Montini wrote for the periodical *Studium* in 1930–1931, in an article where his core vision of the Church faced with the modern world first started to take shape. It came to fruition years later in his Encyclical Letter *Ecclesiam Suam*. In these early writings, Montini puts the focus on the Apostle Paul, seeing in him not only a stubbornness to defend the truth of the Christian faith, but, on the basis of this truth, to better express its university and capacity to be proclaimed and accepted by everyone:

> … both aspects of apostolic tolerance, that is, faith's universality and particularity, are derived from the typical attitude of Christians toward non-Christians. Such an attitude has never been hostile, unsympathetic, or closed in on itself, but rather full of understanding and eager for friendship, ready to assimilate the good and make it more fruitful wherever it is found. Neither does

this tendency toward tolerance stem from a lazy acquiescence to a world it thinks cannot be healed or from an egotistical refusal to fight for the cause of Christ; neither is it cowardice or an "ostrich" approach to life where one buries his or her head in the sand whenever there is an impending threat, pretending it doesn't exist. Rather, the Christian view takes a wide, liberal, optimistic vision of the world based on a criterion of mercy, which Christianity introduces to the world in order to heal it. It is a supernatural trust in the redemptive power of the Gospel applicable to every condition in life; in short, it is a sort of "apologetic relativism."

This passage reveals the lucidity and foresight of Montini's vision. He describes the Church's relationship with the world in light of the persuasive power of the Gospel truth which, together with mercy, penetrates the human heart in order to tear it away from a sinful state.

Along the same lines, the thought of a faith lived by witness and made stronger by credibility is a reflection Msgr Montini deepened in the 1950s:

My friends, I invite you, above all, to consider the beauty of our act of faith ... it would take too long to show all the objections that arose in the soul of a twentieth-century intellectual when invited to make an act of faith. The modern spirit has been taught to doubt and criticize. It is used to considering its own dignity along the lines of its own autonomy and independence. It prefers the little light of its own intelligence to the light a higher intelligence could give it. It is proud of its own uncertainties, its own sufferings, its own errors... the act of faith is not irrational by any means. Being above reason, it presupposes it, needs it, supports it, strengthens it: *intelligo ut credam, credo ut intelligam.* It would be extremely interesting to see how Saint Anselm's ancient formulae might be adapted to the conditions of temporary thought in order to show that reason, in its manifold aspects, precedes faith, in such a way that what the Church has adopted and, so to speak, canonized, is nothing but a form of enlightened, human, solid "intellectualism," entirely concerned with the dictates of logic and objectivity ... faith is a form of strength. It is a strength because it is a grace, a virtue. It is a strength because it obliges the human spirit to a deep and coherent understanding of its conditions. It is a strength because it requires a supreme and balanced use of man's spiritual faculties, intelligence and will. It is a strength because it reveals life's ultimate meaning and pushes man to take on new and challenging responsibilities, forcing him to use an impeccable moral logic: *iustus ex fide vivet.* There is no true holiness that does not emanate from faith ... Faith is a strength because it urges us on to action beyond the "Catholic" world and into the world at large. The world at large is also dedicated to action; but because of its weakness and vulnerability it seems to have become a giant when it comes to practical activity, but in a way that the exigencies and methods of action have taken the place of the principles of thought.

In this context, the testimony of Paul VI's personal secretary, Msgr Macchi, is of particular value: "Essentially Paul VI's life revolved around the task of safeguarding the deposit of faith, but doing it in such a way that its contents would be understood more readily and thus more easily accessible to the modern world." As we can see, the *fil rouge* that constantly guided Paul VI was a faith serving as an assurance for believers, who have a need to be continually rooted in it more deeply. Furthermore, this is something possible for *everybody*, because the truth contained and transmitted through faith is a condition of humanity without which existence would not find anything that truly corresponded to it. In the throes of the youth movement of 1968, the Pope could say with utmost confidence:

> Do not be afraid! Have faith! Yes, it is still possible to believe in God and in Christ today. Now is a better time than ever to have faith in God, given that human intelligence is more highly developed, more educated toward thinking, more inclined to search for the innermost and ultimate reasons for each and every thing.

Pope Montini was radically immersed in this perspective of faith, which required steadfastness and fidelity for its nourishment. This is shown in a commentary on the Second Letter of Paul to Timothy he had written as a young man in the 1920s and 1930s. Echoes of this text can be found in his episcopal teaching and Petrine ministry, almost as if it were a clarion call to a path which he had been preparing for a long time:

> Given the general loss of truth and a lack of taste for truth, the Bishop must be a firm and zealous teacher. He must reconcile a firmness and a liveliness of teaching. The faith is preserved by confessing it; it is spread by affirming it; and it lives by defending it; it should have no other effect than to stimulate a more active, convincing, and effective teaching.

Constancy in hope

A faith of this kind must be animated by a hope that offers certainty and does not disappoint. Paul VI, as many have testified, lived — as he definitely lived the last decade of his life — "in a spirit of internal, spiritual contemplation enabling him to see everything *sub specie aeternitatis*; in a spirit of prayer and self-sacrifice that could only have come from a deep and intimate immersion in the life of God." It was with these words that the Cardinal Vicar, Ugo Poletti, explained his own perception of Paul VI's lifestyle. In one of his writings from the 1930s, we find a description of the hope that not only describes Paul VI's theological conception of this virtue, but how he tried to live it out concretely in his own life:

> Christian hope is not simply a presupposition, a conjecture, or a desire ... it is to prop oneself up with a reality, a presence, an assistance, a divine intervention, which can never fail or fall short ... it is an optimism born from his hope; a hope that is not based on our strength, but is there for us as a *must*.

I believe this certitude of hope was constantly present within him, especially because he always carried within him the thought of death. It is interesting to read what Msgr Macchi has to say on this topic:

> Pope Paul VI was taught, and in fact he taught others, to think about death. He was taught to live with sickness and a desire to make use of the time the Lord gave him to enrich his soul with meditation, and also to complete quickly and intensely all the good he could possibly accomplish ... The thought of death for him, as he himself had written in a meditation on death, was not a reality that saddened him. It was

> rather a thought that stirred him to action, as
> he himself used to say, to do good, to do it right
> away; to do everything that was still left to do
> with enthusiasm before the Lord came again
> and called us to the glory of heaven.

This kind of thinking sometimes urged Paul VI to remark how beautiful it would be to meet the Lord definitively on the day of the Transfiguration. In fact, the episode on Mount Tabor had been for a long time something Paul VI reflected on in his mediation and prayer. The Lord accepted this desire and called him to himself exactly on the liturgical feast of the Transfiguration. Msgr Magee confirms this personal desire of the Pope: "toward the end of this life, the Servant of God often said to me that he knew death was approaching, but that he hoped he would have the joy of presenting himself to the Lord precisely on the Solemnity of the Transfiguration. And, as providence would have it, that was precisely when he died." This feast day corresponded to a personal devotion the Pope had cultivated for a long time. There are several pieces of evidence for this. The first is that August 6th was the publication of his first Enclycical, *Ecclesiam Suam*, in 1964. Furthermore, it was he who suggested that the apse of the chapel of the Lombard Seminary should be decorated with the scene of Mount Tabor. Finally, in his book *Thoughts on Death*, everything becomes clearer in the light of an attitude of prayer that gives support and strength to his thinking:

> *Ambulate dum lucem habetis* (Jn 12:35). This is
> everything: in the end, I would like to be in the
> light. Usually the end of life on this earth, if it
> is not obscured by sickness, has a sort of foggy
> clarity: a clarity of memories, of beautiful

things, attractive things, unfinished things,
nostalgic things, and things so clear that by now
we don't have to be anxious about their irre-
trievability and we can scoff at their summons
to desperation. There is a light that enlightens
the disillusionment of a life found on ephemeral
goods and failed hopes. There is the light of
vague and useless regrets. There is the light of
wisdom that finally shows the vanity of things
and the value of virtues that should have
characterized the course of one's life: *vanitas
vanitatum*. As for me, in the end I would like to
have a synthetic and wise view of the world and
life: I believe that such a notion should be
expressed in a kind of recognition: everything
was a gift, everything was a grace; and how
beautiful the panoramic view it gave me;
simply too beautiful, to the point that it allured
and enchanted us, even though it should have
appeared to us as a sign and an invitation. But,
in any case, it seems that the farewell should be
expressed in a majestic though simple act of
acknowledgement, indeed of gratitude: this
mortal life, despite its trails, its obscure
mysteries, its sufferings, and its tragic fallen-
ness, is a beautiful thing, a marvel ever-new and
moving, an event worth singing about joyfully
and in glory: the life, the life of man!

In short, for Pope Montini the Transfiguration was an
iconic vision of a life worth living to the full. Indeed,
it was Peter himself who attested, "Lord, it is good for
us to be here" (*Mk* 9:5). The successor of Peter could
not help but make this experience his own and to see
it as a fulfilment of his own hope.

His ardent hope is all the more significant if we
consider the controversies within the Church surround-

ing his person and his Pontificate. It was precisely the certitude of his faith that led him to place ever more strongly his unshaken trust in the salvific and redemptive action of Christ. The Pope was an expert communicator of this hope as attested by Doctor A. Pignatelli, who went to Montini for spiritual direction:

> The hope of the Servant of God was constantly visible in his ongoing serenity of spirit, which was particularly evident whenever he or I was experiencing difficulty. I never saw the Servant of God discouraged. In his spiritual direction, whenever I was having difficulties, he would invite me to hope, to perseverance, to abandonment and trust in God who is "faithful in his promises."

Finally, it should be clear that the certainty of this hope shatters any myth about the doubts and uncertainties surrounding Giovanni Battista Montini and his Pontificate and any attempt to depict him as a Hamlet figure incapable of decision. A letter of Msgr Macchi clears away any doubt to this effect:

> Although there are those who view the Servant of God as a sad, indecisive, and anxious figure, I would like to affirm that Paul VI was always profoundly serene. This was precisely because his hope was always lively, even when faced with the gravest problems besetting the Church and society ... Whenever his face appeared sad or tense, it was not due to a lack of hope or trust in divine providence, but rather he empathized deeply with the realities that afflicted mankind and the Church.

It should come as no surprise that in his life, as in anyone's life, there were moments of genuine sadness. Yet sadness is not opposed to sanctity. He saw the

world as divided into two "blocks": the explosive
violence that led to the death of Aldo Moro, one of the
young students who went through the experience of
FUCI with Msgr Montini; the protests and marches of
young people who challenged traditional values and
overturned or discarded them; the confusion of the
Church in the West, together with its persecution in
eastern Europe: none of this could have left a normal
person in peace, let alone the successor of Peter, whose
very vocation is to shoulder willingly the weight of
humanity. Paul VI's sadness, to repeat, did not oppose
his holiness, because it was not without hope. With
this hope, sadness is a form of participation in the
suffering of mankind. Sadness and tears were also
present in the life of Jesus, but these did not lessen his
unconditional trust in the Father and in His love. To
fall into sadness for the sin of men and their violent
tendencies is a strong clarion call to be vigilant in
sustaining both faith and hope in the progressive
realization of the plan of salvation God has realized
for the Church and for the world whenever it cooper-
ates with His grace. Indeed, Pope Paul VI was very
fond of repeating this refrain: "I entrust everything to
the Lord." His episcopal motto was *In nomine Domini*,
an expression that was anything but rhetorical, but
rather indicative of the path of life and the ideal he
wanted to pursue constantly.

Diligent in charity

As far as regards Paul VI's charity, I marveled at a
remark Cardinal A. Casaroli made in his testimony:
"Without having any concrete anecdotes to give regarding this point, it was always very clear to me in the way

Paul VI behaved and spoke that he was deeply in love with God." I can sympathize with the Cardinal's hesitation to give concrete examples of charity since they are infinite in the life of Paul VI and well known. Perhaps they have been too quickly forgotten, but this does not make them any less significant. We only have to think of his expressed desire to sell real estate owned by the Holy See in the center of Rome in order to fund housing projects for needy families in Acilia on the outskirts of Rome. This act has not been forgotten since that section of the city still bears the name *Villaggio Paolo VI* in commemoration of his generosity. But there are many, many more testimonies that converge unanimously on the Pope's extraordinary love: a love that became the very reason for sharing the pain and suffering of others. The suffering of the then-Cardinal Montini was well known when, returning from Mantova, where he had presided over the funeral of Msgr Domenico Manna, the Bishop of that diocese, his driver accidently hit an eighteen-year-old boy, Pier Luigi Cessi, while he was making a hazardous move on his bicycle. Pier Luigi was immediately found to be in serious condition and was taken to the hospital in Bozzolo in the Archbishop's own car. He died shortly thereafter. The letter Montini wrote to Father Primo Mazzolari shows how deeply he shared the family's grief and suffering in the wake of this tragedy:

> To the dear Reverend Fr Primo Mazzolari,
>
> I have sent Msgr Luigi Adani, Vicar General of the Archdiocese of Milan, together with my secretary, Fr Pasquale Macchi, to represent me at the funeral of Pier Luigi Cessi, as they have promised to convey my condolences and a pledge of prayers to you and everyone present

at the funeral ceremony. But I would ask you, the spiritual father of the bereaved, to please tell his parents, his sister, his loved ones, and all those who are bereaving over his lifeless body that I too am crying, I too am suffering, I too am praying with them. Oh my! How this tragedy weighs heavily on my heart, how confounded I am by the mystery of its sense-lessness. My heart cries out: "no, this should never have happened, it should never have been this way!" I hear my soul quaking, asking, "why, why?" I think you will know, Father, how to tell all of those mourning—and espe-cially the Mom and Dad of Pier Gorgio—that he was good: that he also has a Father in heaven, such that even the earth-shattering and inexplicable events of this world hide the secret of providence and goodness which will be revealed to us someday, and that now places on our lips the humble but magnificent words, "God's will be done!" And please speak to them of paradise, of the life that never dies, and of the family of Saints. And please tell them that I will always carry Pier Luigi in my heart; and that I would like to impart to all my pastoral blessing as a sign of comfort and strength.

The testimony of Cardinal J. Willebrands particularly highlights the extraordinary love of blessed Paul VI:

In the person of Paul VI, it would be hard to separate his service to the Church from his love for the Church. His service sprang from his love; he was replete with love to the core. He loved the Church in his work, in people, in his prayer, in Rome, in Milan, and in his travels.

Montini allowed himself to be guided by love and the logic of love as he strove to give his entire self without expecting anything in return. He proposed love as the catalyst for building up a "civilization of love," the main protagonist on the international stage as he taught in his encyclical *Populorum Progressio,* and it was love that inspired him to apply the phrase "the greatest duty of charity" to Catholics entrusted with political responsibility. A clear indication that Paul VI had not suddenly concocted a life of charity but prepared for it for a long time emerges from the testimony of Cardinal U. Poletti, whom Paul VI chose to be the Vicar of Rome: "He would not have cultivated the kind of charity evident in both the little and big things of his Pontificate if he had not been nourished by it from his youth, day by day. From charity and prayer, exercised with great patience, he built up the edifice of his life." As confirmation of this vision, we can turn to the testimony of His Excellency Msgr Carlo Manziana, who was a regular visitor of Montini for many years: "His love for the poor was zealous, present from the days of his youth, and it only got stronger over time as his pastoral responsibilities increased."

A final word about his exercise of the theological virtues might be offered by way of synthesis. We could relate page after page of testimony proving his authentic possession of and exercise of faith, hope, and love. But there is one word that undergirds them all: *consistency.* Paul VI was a person who chose to live the faith with profound consistency, fully aware of the freedom he enjoyed as a human person. He lived the theological virtues with a conviction and intensity, and he became an eloquent spokesperson for these virtues: not because of the ministry he was obliged to perform as a priest, bishop, and Pope, but more fundamentally because he was enthusiastically convinced of the serenity of soul and the peace that the theological virtues give in response to the search for meaning that percolates in the heart of every human being.

In addition to numerous testimonies that paint his life of sanctity, I would like to add one personal memory of my own. The television carried live the events of Paul VI's coronation. I was only a twelve-year-old boy, but I will never forget the Pope's gestures greeting the ecstatic crowds as he passed by. You could see from his face that he was emotional but also happy as he blessed the people from his *sedia gestatoria,* swaying to and fro while carried by the chair-bearers. At a certain point, you could hear the strong voice of the Cardinal ring out as he held up a cotton ball, set it aflame, and watched it immediately die out: *"Pater Sancte, sic transit gloria mundi."* I was just a young lad, but I can still see Paul VI's face in front of me. Up to that point the new Pontiff had looked festive and content. But then, at those words, he became serious, quite serious. He reflected intensely on that eloquent symbol and remained absorbed in it for some time. I don't know what was going through his head at that moment. I only know it struck me to see his face showed without a doubt his awareness of the gravity of the office to which he had been elected and the responsibility it would entail. That moment brings to mind such humility and magnanimity combined in one man. He was able to grasp the true meaning of the Petrine ministry and he wanted to apply himself to carrying it out with his whole existence, ready to give his life for it. Finally, let us turn to the testimony of his successor in the See of Milan, Cardinal C. M. Martini:

> I could always see in him a profound believer, humble, open and attentive to dialogue, ready

to assist but afraid of disturbing others, a person with an extraordinary gift or perseverance under trial. I am certain that the example of his life will help many to place the search for sanctity at the center of their lives.

4

BEYOND THE DIFFICULTIES

HE CAUSE FOR beatification does not merely involve a candidate's positive characteristics such as the living out of the theological virtues. A considerable part of the process is also dedicated to the candidate's problematic side, his limits, his short-comings, and how they might impede him from living sanctity to the full. A Blessed will be offered up as an example for all to follow, so the Church must make every effort to inspect all aspects of the individual's life. A Blessed or a Saint certainly remains imbedded in his or her humanity. Saints are not perfect persons, but rather men and women who strove to live the Gospel faithfully and consistently with all their strength, sustained by the grace of God even though they continued to show signs of their natural weaknesses. Such considerations are all the more important if the candidate is a pope. The interwoven fabric of a life of sanctity and the exercise of the Petrine mission is very complicated and intricate. Sometimes the two threads combine in an inextricable way, and at other times it is necessary to tease them out from one another. Certainly, when it comes to "politics" and to the consequences of one's personal actions, we cannot perfectly distinguish the two, but neither are they identical. The holiness of Paul VI, as with any other pope, cannot be judged solely on the basis of his Pontificate. To make a historical judgment on any Pontificate is a multifaceted and complex task because it involves many other persons and historical circumstances that cannot be linked to the successor of Peter alone.

As far as regards the specific case of Paul VI, it is worth pointing out that the paperwork of his cause consisted of more than 4,700 pages. A part of this comprises the work of the historical commission. Consisting of Professors F. A. Sullivan, G. Giachi, G. Mucci, C. Caprile, and L. Bogliolo, its task was to verify the validity of the historicity of the writings attributed to Giovanni Battista Montini in order to formulate a judgment on their doctrinal soundness. One remark of the commission is particularly worth noting:

> The historical experts ... unanimously agree that they are dealing with an extraordinary, complex, multifaceted person. They recognize they are standing on the threshold of an internal world that is profound, unfathomable, as well as simply, essentially, consistently, and persistently evangelic, offering an inestimable legacy and gift to the world.

In addition to their work, there is the documented testimony of 169 witnesses: 76 in Rome, 71 in Milan, and 22 in Brescia. The picture one gets from reading their testimonies is very impressive, especially because it is a wide-ranging group of personalities and professions. 28 cardinals were called to testify, 17 bishops, as well as priests, lay men and women, and men and women religious. All of them knew Paul VI personally during different phases of his life. To this list we need to add 36 other testimonies that the Bishop of Brescia, Msgr Morstabilini, had authorized and collected so that they wouldn't be lost with the passing of the years since they dealt with the first decade of Paul VI's life. This brings us to an impressive number of 205 testimonies covering the entire lifespan of Pope Montini. This enables us to assemble a full mosaic of his life, each tile consisting of a single testimony, together representing a man whose life left an indelible mark on the Church in the twentieth century. This collection of testimonies also gives us access to the critiques directed against him and which would have constituted an impediment to his sanctity. It is worth taking a closer look at this evidence because it actually gives us fuel for countering the criticisms and verifying, inasmuch as possible, the course of events and the role Paul VI played in their development. In fact, the critiques touch on various aspects of Paul VI's life that are quite different and had various levels of influence on his legacy. They have been interpreted in different ways, but in the end it is possible to reconstruct their most salient features and, most of all, to ascertain the role played by the Pope. More specifically, these are the points that were treated:

1. The relationship between Pius XII and the nomination of Montini to Milan;

2. The interpretation of the collegiality of bishops and the primacy of the High Pontiff in the redaction of the *Nota praevia* amended to the Dogmatic Constitution *Lumen Gentium*;

3. The liturgical reform called for by the Second Vatican Council;

4. The question of *Humanae Vitae*;

5. His involvement with certain problems in the
    Church in Holland;

6. His relationship with Spain, and especially with
    General Francisco Franco;

7. The Italian law on divorce and the referendum.

To sort through these issues successfully, one must not
get caught up in the morass of interpretations and
opinions that were in vogue at the time but lacking a
solid historical basis or documentation. Rather, the
specific task during a cause for beatification is to attest
to the exercise of virtue by Pope Montini and his ability
to live the faith consistently in the midst of these
difficult circumstances. We must also not forget that
many of these questions are of a "political" character
and, as such, will always be clouded by controversial
interpretations based on the preconceptions of those
who undertake the difficult task of reconstructing the
facts. What we can do, however, is approach the
objective facts as closely as possible to understand the
actual behavior of Paul VI with constant reference to
his life of the theological virtues and his sanctity. There
are limits inherent in the sources available to us, but
we must also rely on the testimony of persons directly
involved in the events.

Montini in Milan

The first question regards the nomination of Montini
as Archbishop of Milan by Pope Pius XII. This appointment has sometimes been interpreted as a maneuver
to distance the then-Secretariat of State from Rome.
According to this interpretation, the diverging political
opinions of Montini and Pius XII persuaded the latter

to free himself of his collaborator whom he trusted less and less. Actually, this is not the only possible interpretation. Granted, it is clear that Montini and Pius XII had increasingly differing opinions on political questions such as the role of Christian Democrats. But we cannot ignore another, more likely, motive for the appointment to Milan. Pius XII wanted Montini, who up until that moment had not had extensive pastoral experience, to gain some experience in preparation for future responsibilities. Both these interpretations are quite possible and have a historical basis. One can prefer one or the other, but one cannot deny that they make up a single, complex whole. In the first place, what is known for sure is that the so-called "Roman party," the head of which was the then-rector of the Major Seminary of Rome, Monsignor Ronca, did not have a high regard for Montini's actions. Montini, in fact, did not hesitate to use his political connections to initiate an eventual dialogue with the communists to deliberate ways to develop the political system in Rome and in Italy. Neither can we forget the action of Gedda, the then-president of Catholic Action, who had ready access to Pius XII and had the willing ear of the Pope. Gedda's collaborator, Adele Pignatelli, clarifies this relationship in her testimony:

> In the period following the war, those involved with Catholic Action knew well the suffering that Prof. Luigi Gedda caused Msgr Montini. Gedda's ideas were very different from Montini's. Through my involvement with the Young Women's movement in Catholic Action, I knew first-hand that Prof. Luigi Gedda turned repeatedly to Pius XII, imposing his point of view, which was different and sometimes diametrically opposed to decisions taken by Msgr Montini, the

then-Pro-Secretary of State. I think this could
have had an effect on the relationship between
Pope Pius XII and the Servant of God, who for
his part was always very respectful of every
decision made by His Holiness.

Gedda was certainty not favorable to Montini, and
could even be downright hostile. We also cannot
underestimate the significance of the resignation of the
Vice President of the Youth Branch of Catholic Action
(G.I.A.C.), Mario Rossi, who succeeded Carlo Carretto
in 1952, who, out of opposition to president Gedda,
had abandoned the Youth Branch of Catholic Action.
Montini tried to intervene to slow down the process
and convince Rossi to change his mind. But the whole
thing blew up precisely due to the young Rossi's
opposition to Gedda.

Finally, it is also important to consider the friendship between Montini and Father De Luca. De Luca, a
priest of Rome, had a razor-sharp intellect and ability
to network extensively with many different people,
including politicians distant from the Church. Being
privy to these relationships allowed Montini to take a
much wider view of the political scene at the time. De
Luca, however, because of his lifestyle and personality,
was not admired in many sectors of the Curia. When
we put all these factors together, more credence is
given to the thesis that Montini, the pro-Secretary of
State, was nominated to Milan precisely to distance
him from Rome. But the question is not so much what
Pius XII's intention was in nominating Montini to the
Archdiocese of Milan, but rather how the latter viewed
the nomination and reacted to it. He certainly looked
at it with suffering. After many years of direct service
to the Holy Father, it was hard for him to picture what

it would be like to be away from him. But the biggest reason for his suffering was the prospect of having to begin a whole new pastoral assignment, not to mention one as demanding as the Archdiocese of Milan, without ever having had pastoral experience like this before. His biggest fear and worry was that he would not be up to the task. This is clear in a letter he wrote to the then-Substitute of the Secretariat of State, Msgr A. dell'Acqua, a great friend of his: "I seem to be dreaming. I have to convince myself again and again that this really *is* my responsibility. As long as it is the will of God, as long as it is the Holy Father's wish! I am going in with eyes closed."

In any case, Montini's service as Archbishop of Milan provided him with invaluable pastoral experience. His time in the largest diocese in the world, his tireless work on behalf of its parishes and the construction of new ones, the reorganization of the diocese to ensure that newly developed zones of the city would be ministered to, the launching of a mission in 1957 to those "far off" —a term he used to designate those in need of hearing the Gospel and a reassurance of the Church's closeness to them –carried out in a true *religious sense* as indicated in his pastoral letter for Lent that year: all these events prepared Montini thoroughly for the great adventure of the Petrine ministry by giving him a more solid and well-rounded experience. We cannot deny that, during those years, some actions taken by people very close to Pius XII were not always viewed as favorable to the Archbishop of Milan. Disrespect and malevolence stemming from the Curia were aimed at him. Montini's way of reacting, however, was never anything less that obedience and fidelity to the successor or Peter, whom he always considered a father-figure and friend.

The Nota Praevia *in* Lumen Gentium

A second problem regards Paul VI's views regarding episcopal collegiality and the preparation of the *Nota Praevia* in Chapter III of the Dogmatic Constitution on the Church, *Lumen Gentium.* It has been alleged that the inclusion of this note went beyond his authority of governance. The suggestion is that he weakened the notion of Petrine Primacy taught by the First Vatican Council, and that he did not issue the teaching on collegiality in a doctrinally clear manner. But as any careful analysis of *Lumen Gentium,* the *Nota Praevia,* and Paul VI's speeches at the conclusion of the conciliar sessions will reveal, the criticisms directed against his decision were nothing but manipulative and fail to reflect his true mind and intention. In fact, the critics are convinced that the pope betrayed the Church's traditional teaching on the primacy of the successor of Peter. But such a criticism is entirely unjustified and, in many respects, falls victim to the same error made by many who view Vatican II in strict discontinuity with the teaching of the Council of Trent. Nothing, in fact, is more unjustified and unjustifiable than to read Paul VI's decision as a break with the preceding tradition. To the contrary, his entire teaching and action fully accord with the preceding tradition, and the texts themselves confirm it. The assiduous and vigilant attention he gave to safeguarding doctrine leaves little room for doubt about his intentions. It is enough to look at a few passages from his speeches to verify directly what he thought and what his convictions were.

On September 29th, 1963, during his speech for the opening of the second session of the Council, he said:

> The Church's conscience is made clear by adhering with unswerving fidelity to the words and affirmations of Christ, by receiving with reverent respect the sure teachings of the Sacred Tradition, by assenting to the internal illuminations of the Holy Spirit, who now seems to ask this of the Church: that with all her strength she would strive to help all people see what she is. I think this wish is being fulfilled: namely, that in this Ecumenical Council the Spirit of truth shed its most radiant light on the sacred Orders of the teaching Church and that He inspire the most evident teaching on the nature of the Church, and that in this way it is certified that the Spouse of Christ is looking at him for its model and, moved by a most ardent love for Him, she may strive to discover her true form; that is, the beauty He wishes to emit through His Church ... Among the many and varied problems that will be discussed in this Council, first and foremost will be your own role as Bishops of the Church of God. We do not hesitate to assure you that we are anticipating that discussion with great hope and sincere trust. Practically speaking, while giving due regard for the dogmatic declarations made concerning the Roman Pontiff at the First Ecumenical Vatican Council, a deeper teaching will have to be formulated on the Episcopate, its duties, and its relationship to Peter. For this reason, criteria will also emerge as to how We are to carry out the apostolic mission entrusted to Us. This universal office, even though Christ has endowed it with a complete and adequate authority of power, will have to mature and

expand its capacity to assist and collaborate if Our Brothers in the Episcopate are to offer us more effective and conscientious collaboration in the duties We have assumed and in ways and forms to be opportunely decided upon ... The Council undoubtedly calls for a more fruitful renewal of the Church. At the same time, we must be aware that, from the very fact that we affirm and desire such things, some will say we are exposing the Church to the accusation that she has violated the intention of Her Founder in such an important area. To the contrary, to have established more clearly her fidelity to Christ in regard to essential things is something that fills her with sure and humble joy, and implants within her an eagerness to wipe away the stains of human weakness. The renewal the Council has in mind does not consist in turning the Church's present life upside down or in breaking with her traditions with regard to what is essential and venerable, but rather to respect those traditions and free them from any ephemeral and distorted forms, wanting to render them authentic and fruitful.

Another significant text is the speech the Pope gave at the end of the second session, on December 4th, 1963:

The crucial and complex question of the Episco-pate, which, both because of the logical treatment it must be given and because of the importance of the topic itself, is the first matter of business of this Second Ecumenical Vatican Council, which, we must not deny, is the natural continuation and completion of the First Ecumenical Vatican Council. The present Council, in no way challenging but rather affirming the prerogatives of the Supreme

Pontiff as deriving explicitly from Christ himself and furnished with every authority needed for the governance of the universal Church, will try to shed light on the nature and function of the Episcopate as willed by God according to the teaching of Our Lord Jesus Christ and the authentic ecclesial tradition, and to establish what its powers are and how they are exercised both in reference to the Bishops taken singly and to them as a whole; in such a way that the lofty ministry of Bishops in the Church of God may be effectively illustrated, not treating it as an autonomous institution independent of the Supreme Pontificate of Peter, much less opposed to it, but rather directed, harmoniously with it and under it, to the common good and the ultimate end of the Church. It will thus come about that by combining our strengths, the hierarchical composition of the Church will be reinvigorated, not attenuated; the internal collaboration will increase, not decrease; the apostolic efficacy will mature, not wilt; and mutual charity will be fervent, not stagnant. Therefore, we trust that the Council, as hoped, will fully clarify and bring to completion this matter of such great importance.

Moreover, on September 14th, at the opening of the third session of the Council, Paul VI once again returned to the topic of the Episcopate with vigor, well aware that the council fathers were dealing with a question of fundamental importance for Church teaching:

The treatment of this doctrine remains to be completed: namely, to explain Christ's will regarding all of His Church, particularly on the nature and function of the successors of the Apostles, that is, the Episcopate, the dignity and

duty of which, through God's goodwill, falls to
you, dear Fathers, or rather to *us*, Most Reverend
Brothers. There are many other things the
Council must discuss, but discussion on this
topic seems to have the greatest importance and
seems to be the most intricate. This very theme
will be remembered for years to come as the
characteristic note of this solemn Council: a
Council which itself is worthy of the historical
annals. It is the task of this Council to resolve
several difficult theological questions: to
examine the nature and sacred function of the
Church's Pastors; to discuss the prerogatives that
legitimately derive from the Episcopate, and,
through the work of the Holy Spirit, to pass a
careful judgment upon them; to delineate the
relationship between this Holy See and the
Bishops; to show that the institutions and forms
of the Church are of the same nature in East and
West, each with its own distinctive peculiarities;
and finally to show the Catholic faithful and our
separated brethren the true notion of the orders
of the holy hierarchy, of which these words have
been said: "The Holy Spirit has appointed you
shepherds to pasture the Church of God (*Acts*
20:28), endowing it with a certain authority that
cannot be placed into doubt. Therefore, bishops
must seek to serve their brothers and sisters
humbly and patiently, as is proper to Pastors,
that is, to ministers of faith and charity.

Finally, at the conclusion of the third session of the
Council, on November 21st, 1964, in a speech summa-
rizing the work of the Council completed up to that
point, the Pope expressed himself in no uncertain terms:

We desire to say only this: We are happy the
doctrine has been handled with enthusiasm,

analysis, and discussion, and that sharp,
pointed conclusions have emerged from those
discussions. It was in fact necessary to complete
the work of Vatican I. The opportune moment
had arrived for several reasons: because of the
recent explosion of theological studies, the
spread of the Catholic Church throughout the
world, the problems that arrive from everyday
pastoral activity which are now presented to
the Church at large, and finally, because of the
desire of many Bishops awaiting a clarification
of the Church's exact teaching in this regard.
The system adopted to complete this task was
also effective: so much so that we hesitate in no
way—when we consider the attached explana-
tions to both interpret the adopted terms, as
well as the theological weight to be attributed
to the proposed doctrine according to the mind
of the Council—I repeat, we do not hesitate to
promulgate, with God's help, this Constitution
on the Church. The best indication that this
promulgation is opportune is that it has not
changed *in any way* the traditional teaching.
What Christ wanted, we too want. What has
preceded us still remains in effect. That which
the Church has taught through the centuries,
we continue to teach. With this difference alone:
that which was contained previously only in its
way of living is now manifestly expressed in its
teaching; that which until now was subject to
reflection and discussion and, in part, to controversy, is now distilled into a precise, doctrinal
formula. We can therefore affirm that by the
intervention of the all-provident God, this
bright hour has dawned on us; an hour, we
would say, whose happening yesterday is
slowly approaching, whose brightness shines

today, whose saving power tomorrow will
certainly enrich the life of the Church with a
progression in doctrine, with more active
strength, with more efficient institutions.

As can be noted from this explicit citation of texts, Paul
VI had a clear idea of the need to treat the topic of
primacy and episcopal collegiality, and he was stead-
fastly determined to ensure that nothing in the Tradition would ever be altered. In this context, it is not out
of place to reconsider the teaching of Benedict XVI in
regard to the correct interpretation of conciliar texts.
In a certain way, his teaching is the most adequate
response to the criticisms and diatribes aimed at Paul
VI. In his famous speech to the Roman Curia in 2005,
Benedict XVI said:

> Well, it all depends on the correct interpretation
> of the Council or—as we would say today—on
> its proper hermeneutics, the correct key to its
> interpretation and application. The problems in
> its implementation arose from the fact that two
> contrary hermeneutics came face to face and
> quarreled with each other. One caused confu-
> sion, the other, silently but more and more
> visibly, bore and is bearing fruit.

On the one hand, there is an interpretation that I would
call "a hermeneutic of discontinuity and rupture"; it has
frequently availed itself of the sympathies of the mass
media, and also one trend of modern theology. On the
other, there is the "hermeneutic of reform", of renewal
in the continuity of the one subject-Church which the
Lord has given to us. She is a subject which increases
in time and develops, yet always remaining the same,
the one subject of the journeying People of God.

In short, conciliar teaching was proposed with such continuity and consistency in doctrine that we can perceive a progression of dogma and its development without any type of alteration.

The liturgical reform

A third question regards the controversy surrounding the reform of the liturgy. Criticisms in this camp stem from a radical polemic advanced by a few bishops who refused to accept the liturgical reforms of the Council. The substance of their criticisms revolve around a few key points: the use of the vernacular, the *Ordo Missae*, the Offertory Rite, the new Eucharistic prayers, the liturgical calendar, and the removal of the octave of Pentecost. With regard to the cause for Paul VI's sanctity, there were a few witnesses who placed the Pope's prudence and vigilance into question, especially in the way he dealt with the then-Secretary of the Commission for the reform of the liturgy in conformity with the dictates of the Council, Father Annibale Bugnini. However, close analysis of the documents reveals that Paul VI was assiduously attentive and concerned about the process of reform. An initial fact to consider is that, already by the time he was Archbishop of Milan, Montini showed his desire that the Council approve the use of the vernacular language in the liturgy, except for the canon which should remain in Latin. Montini retained this stance, entirely deemed legitimate, until the very end, remaining in full accord with the conciliar guidelines. What we can glean from the documents is that at the end of the Council, Montini made an agreement with the German and Dutch Bishops that they could also

translate the canon—as permitted by Vatican II—in
the case where the faithful would grasp the liturgy
more easily as a result. In fact, it happened that many
bishops throughout the world followed the practice
implemented in Holland and began a *de facto* celebration of the liturgy in the vernacular. This, however, did
not occur so much as a direct result of the Pope as by
the application of a conciliar teaching applied by the
Bishops. In any case, the question itself is not of a
dogmatic character nor does the use of the vernacular
betray the Tradition. The presence of other liturgical
languages, much older than Latin, clearly attests that
the Church lived out her life using a wide range of
languages. Furthermore, we must consider that Paul
VI wrote to Father Bugnini in his own hand to com-
plain about the loss of the Octave of Pentecost. The
latter replied to the Pope with an ample and attentive
response in which he shows that the Octave was a later
liturgical addition, and that its presence is not found
in any text of the Church's first millennium. Furthermore, he suggested that the liturgical scholars who
were experts in this area judged it was better to leave
the question to the competence of the episcopal conferences. Upon receiving this response, and in harmony with Paul VI's sensitivity to, and repeated call
for, a concerted effort to exercise episcopal collegiality,
Montini judged it best not to push the issue any further
and to accept the reforms proposed by the Council.

Finally, it must be admitted that many of the
criticisms aimed at the Pope were in fact due to abuses
perpetrated by others. Indeed, it would have been
difficult for the Pope to intervene effectively in these
matters. Even today, the inappropriateness of many
liturgical decisions is clear for all to see, and eliminat-

ing them is a never-ending battle. The prudence, pastoral sensitivity, and sense of governance exercised by Pope Paul VI appear to have been completely in harmony with his responsibility and character, showing that, even in the case of the liturgy, he not only pursued the task of reform launched by the Council, but was guided and sustained by tireless and tenacious apostolic zeal. One particular text of Montini's clearly brings this out. On December 4th, 1963, at the conclusion of the second session of the Council, he had this to say in regard to the liturgical reform:

> Moreover, our lively and detailed discussions have not borne little fruit: in fact, the topic we first confronted, which in a certain sense is preeminent for the Church because of its nature and dignity—and I mean by that the sacred Liturgy—has come to an auspicious conclusion, and today we happily celebrate in this solemn rite the promulgation of the final document. This gives us great joy. In fact, it is clearly evident that the right order of values and duties has been respected: for we see that the place of honor is reserved to God; and that our duty, above all, is to raise prayers to God; that the sacred Liturgy is the primary font of that divine exchange in which the life of God is communicated to us, it is the primary school of our souls, it is the first gift we must make to the Christian people, united with us in faith and assiduous in prayer; and finally, that the initial invitation to mankind to unloose its tongue in holy and sincere prayers and to feel the incredible regeneration of soul and hope possible when they join us in singing God's praises through Jesus Christ and in the Holy Spirit ... we desire that no one go against the established norms of the

public prayer of the Church by adding their
own individual changes or personal rites; we
desire that no one abrogate to themselves the
power to apply in an arbitrary way the Constitution on the Sacred Liturgy, which we
promulgate today, before the opportune and
fixed norms are published and any modifica-
tions are legitimately approved by the
Commissions to be appointed after the Council.
May this noble prayer of the Church ring out
with concordant voice throughout the world!
May no one upset it or violate it!

Humanae Vitae

A fourth problem regards the encyclical *Humanae Vitae.*
As is well known, it is not a problem easily solved. An
abundance of documentary evidence combined with
a limited knowledge of archival records and a plethora
of interpretations make it even more difficult. The
testimony given by Cardinal Suenens based on his own
archival evidence is crucial. He was one of the most
important figures in the history that led up to *Humanae
Vitae.* During the conciliar sessions, he was one of the
most vocal proponents of adjusting moral principles
in light of this question. He believed that the Church
should avoid making the same error it did centuries
before during the crisis with Galileo Galilei. Paul VI
was well aware of the many difficulties and multifaceted problems the issue entailed. He nonetheless felt
it his duty to intervene and remind everyone of the
Magisterial principles involved. According to some
sources, including the Archbishop of Albi, Dupuy, and
the then-Archbishop of Grenoble, Matagrin, it was the
then-Cardinal Archbishop of Krakow, Karol Wojtyła,

who encouraged Paul VI to intervene. However significant that would be, the sources are scarce, and, in any event, it is not a crucial point to the issue at hand. What we can ascertain with certainty is Paul VI's reaction to Cardinal Suenens' intervention according the latter's own testimony: "It was the worst audience of my life. The Holy Father told me that the conciliar bishops had lost all credit in his eyes ... He was hard, he was trenchant, and there was nothing I could say in response. It all finished with him telling me that he would await my retraction."

Relations between Paul VI and Cardinal Suenens would remain tense for years to come. The Pope clearly wanted to hold the line on the Church's teaching and, with great *parrhesia* and charity, he reminded the Cardinal in various settings that his attitude toward moral doctrine was inappropriate and lacking in collegiality. But Cardinal Suenens did not change his stance. Only when he encountered the Renewal of the Spirit, Chiara Lubich, and the Focolari and left aside his preoccupation with the issue of *Humanae Vitae* did he renew his contacts with Paul VI. But they never rekindled the friendship they had previously. In any case, the evidence contained in his private archives is essential for understanding Paul VI's actions. He clearly regarded the Pope as someone "capable of listening, not acting from political motives, doctrinally sound, courageous in speaking directly and frankly with others, humble and willing to go beyond his personal opinions, patient, and full of goodness." Nevertheless, in the Cardinal's eyes, the Pope "lacked a spirit of collegiality and shared responsibility." It is difficult to say with certainty which of the two was more lacking a sense of collegiality. If Paul VI tried to impose his

opinion autocratically, then Cardinal Suenens was
right. If, however, it was a matter of preserving a
long-standing teaching—even against the opinion of
some bishops—so to perform his Petrine duty respon-
sibly, then the Cardinal Archbishop of Brussels was
wrong. Despite their contrasting opinions, Paul VI's
strength in maintaining a relationship with Cardinal
Suenens is a testimony to his magnanimity. In another
audience, the Pope got down on his knees in front of
Cardinals Suenens and begged him to pardon his
brusqueness in their exchange. What we can deduce
with certainty from these events, however, is that
Montini always kept in mind the condition of Christian
spouses, responsible parenthood, and the reality of
contraceptive methods. He carried out wide consultation on the question, and at the end of the process he
made his decision in continuity with the Church's
preceding Magisterium. Granted, neither did he want
to submit the question to the judgment of the Council
or the Synod of Bishops, as some would have liked, nor
did he follow the majority decision of the Commission
instituted to study the question. And why not? Because
the inquiry was not making headway. It was his pre-
rogative as Supreme Pontiff to handle the question
first-hand in order to prevent a dramatic split within
the College of Bishops. He shouldered the entire responsibility upon himself. Those who maintain that Paul VI
should have handed the question over to the Synod of
Bishops forget that this body is only consultative and
not deliberative, and, for that reason, it had no more
competence than that already entrusted to the Commission. In hindsight, it is easier to appreciate the wisdom
with which Paul VI handled this difficult issue. Scientific studies continue to show that natural family plan-

ning is more conducive to a family's wellbeing and that responsible fatherhood and motherhood is the more effective path to family stability.

The Church in Holland

The fifth problem regards initiatives taken by the Dutch Church. It is easy for us to see today how short-sighted some of these self-appointed reforms were. After half a century, it is easy for us to see how the effects of those reforms, in some cases devastating, deeply upset the people of those local communities. It becomes even more evident when we consider the great task of the new evangelization they are called to undertake within the specific context of widespread secularism.

There are essentially two issues: the *Dutch Catechism* and the *Dutch Pastoral Council.* The history of the catechism is quite complex. Work on it began in 1956, before the Council, and it was concluded in 1966. The explicit aim of the Catechism was to reinterpret Catholic doctrine in the light of the social and cultural circumstances of the modern world. The question of what sort of language would be most appropriate for the catechism arose right away, as well as how modern problems relate to Church doctrine. On the one hand, the new catechism had many merits. On the other hand, it treated some dogmatic points in a cursory way while completely ignoring others. Examples include original sin, the existence of angels, the virginity of Mary, the salvific and redemptive merits of Christ, transubstantiation, and various points of moral doctrine. Paul VI appointed a mixed commission, including members of the Roman Curia and others appointed by the Bishops' Conference, to review the points in question. The work went on for nearly three years but was compromised by the polemical tendencies of some members—including Fr E. Schillebeeckx—and for the manipulative use of social communications—typical of the time—to assert autonomy apart from Rome. Many translations were made of this *Catechism* and they sold with tremendous success. The frenzy for novelty obscured the desire for truth. The *Catechism* had proven to be a highly useful tool for adults. But the partial presentation of the faith watered down the truth of revelation.

Paul VI took a consistent stance toward the problem: he was decisive when necessary, but also respectful of the competency of the local episcopate. After all, he believed strongly in collegiality and would never have exercised his governance in a way that would have contradicted conciliar teaching, especially a teaching he was personally devoted to. We have only to read Pope Montini's various interventions in this affair to understand how his pastoral care and attention was poised between fidelity to the contents of the faith and respect toward his brother bishops.

Something similar occurred with the *Dutch Pastoral Council*. More than once Paul VI petitioned Cardinal Alfrink to give due attention to the proposals being put forth for the local Church, but written records raise the suspicion that there was staunch resistance against any kind of "Roman" intervention. To accuse Paul VI of a lack of governance at that moment seems merely a maneuver to relieve others of responsibility and to deny that governance cannot always be exercised through autocratic decisions, especially in the post-conciliar period when collegiality was brought back to the fore. Furthermore, one has to wonder whether the Holy Father's appeals were taken seriously by the local episcopate and whether continual badgering on his part would have caused greater injury to a sense of ecclesial communion.

Francisco Franco

A sixth problem regards the relationship between Paul VI and General Francisco Franco, as well as the Pope's decision to suspend the cause of beatification and canonization of the Catholic martyrs during the Second Republic and the Civil War. What we must consider above all is the diligent attention Paul VI gave to the Spanish political situation, especially when it came to charging the *Generalissimo* with the death penalty. It is impossible to summarize in a few sentences the political climate in Spain during the Franco regime. What is clear from the documentary evidence is the Spanish bishops' gradual distancing from the regime. The reason Montini's name is linked to the Spanish general is that, while Archbishop of Milan, he had sent a telegram to Franco asking him to revoke the death penalty imposed on some young students accused of terrorism. A few days after the intervention, Montini was elected to the papacy. Consequently his request was not only honored, but "honored" in a wholly new way. Franco suspended the execution of some of the young people but kept it in force for others. This greatly disappointed the Pope who subsequently distanced himself greatly from the regime. After all, given his own solid formation in a spirit of democracy and staunchly opposed to fascism and Nazism, it would have been very difficult for him to accept *Franchismo*. It is one thing to respect the *subjective* feeling of General Franco in professing himself a

Catholic and a son of the Church—something for which Paul VI expressed appreciation and esteem on various occasions—but this is quite different from the political action of the General, something that Pope Montini judged as *ethically* contrary to the principles of Catholic doctrine. It is clear that such an attitude gave birth to the defamation of Paul VI as an enemy of Spain, a friend of the communists, and ready to offend the sentiments of the Spanish people. In any case, when General Franco died, Paul VI took the initiative to launch an effective transition for the Church in Spain. The renewal of the episcopate and his ever-increasing knowledge of and appreciation for the dedication of lay Catholics in Spain's social, political, and cultural life were necessary steps to reach a peaceful conclusion to the turmoil in that country.

As far as regards the suspension of the cause of beatification and canonization of the martyrs, it is worth remembering that Paul VI, in full conformity with Church law, did not want any political party of any persuasion to capitalize on the declaration of martyrdom. For this reason, he asked that the conditions surrounding the death of the candidates be studied with utmost diligence and on the basis of absolutely clear and complete documentation. This does not mean that the merits of the Spanish martyrs went unrecognized, but only that Paul VI judged wisely the need for further, detailed study of the various aspects of their deaths to ascertain effectively the nature of their martyrdom. After all, let us not forget that John Paul II did not initiate a process of beatification for the first Spanish Civil War martyrs until 1987, ten years after elected pope. We know with certainty that on more than one occasion the Church expressed her favorable judgment on such a great witness given by men and women, priests, clerics, bishops, and religious of all ages who gave the Church in Spain a faithful witness of renewal in the Church and its mission in the world today. The delay, therefore, was not due to a lack of willingness or indecision on the part of Paul VI, but rather the need to look for consistent historical material to give a solid basis for the beatification.

Italian law on divorce

The last question is Pope Montini's stance toward the legalization of divorce in Italy. The events leading both to the promulgation of the law and the request to abrogate it through a referendum are well known. The personal dedication of Paul VI in pursuing the issue so closely that he became a "prophetic" sign in society clearly emerges from the available sources. Many testimonies confirm that the Pope, even though he wasn't completely convinced of the favorable outcome of the referendum, made great efforts to ensure that Christian believers would not fall short in their responsibility to involve themselves in an issue of such crucial importance to the good of society. The results of the referendum show that Catholicism was divided, disobedient, and fully taken in by the vortex of secularism which they were called to counter rather than acquiesce to. As G. Andreotti said in his testimony, "The negative result, even though it was not unexpected, deeply troubled Paul VI." The Pope immediately called out to Catholics, asking them not to falter in their witness and direct responsibility to strengthen the institution of marriage, living it fully as a vocation and with consistent and credible commitment.

5

A HEALTHY BABY IS BORN

T WAS QUITE astonishing; I had never seen anything like it before. It was like I was looking at a whole new baby." These were the first words the gynecologist said after looking at one of dozens of sonograms. He knew the case thoroughly and the charts traced a gradual but astonishing transformation week after week. He himself had diagnosed the serious pathology of the fetus in Catherine's womb. At her thirty-first week of pregnancy, the fetus began a precipitous decline that should have ended in immediate death or, at best, a serious birth deformity followed by death. But the situation changed suddenly and completely. Out of respect for the confidentiality of the individuals, I will not cite names and places directly. I shall simply call the baby, "George." When the family and friends submitted their testimony, they requested that their names not be revealed so that they could live in privacy. Such a decision is entirely appropriate since, in my opinion, it only stands as an additional sign of the seriousness of their faith and spirituality. Modern times are marked by a fascination with the faddish, such that everything goes public immediately in the hope of instant fame. So the decision of this family to remain anonymous is all the more laudable. We are obsessed today with divulging and collecting information at the push of a button, posting even the most banal news on Facebook so it can be seen by the largest number of "friends" possible. So the sense of discretion characterizing this family's testimony and their desire to eschew recognition should be welcomed and extoled as a sign of the seriousness of their faith. They are not looking to cause uproar by such an extraordinary event, but rather to give witness by a life of faith that others will naturally want to imitate. It is for this reason that the minute details of the case will not be given, nor any information that might belie the identity of the family. Nevertheless, the miracle in their lives leaves us no less dumbfounded than it did them.

Catherine was a young mother, about thirty years old. As has been customary, she went to visit her gynecologist at the end of the twentieth week of pregnancy to have a sonogram. They wanted to know the sex of the child. It was a happy day. Together with her husband Steve holding their fifteen-month-old daughter Elizabeth, they went to the clinic. Catherine was calm, for it was only a routine exam. Besides, the first pregnancy had gone off without a hitch. There were no problems when she had Elizabeth. The Caesarean section she had was due only to a streptococcus infection causing minor irritation to the fetus, but other than that everything was fine. Why should she have anything to fear this time?

However, the sonogram did not completely satisfy the medical staff. It wasn't clear whether anything was really wrong, so they asked Catherine to come back for another sonogram at the twenty-forth week. It was at that time that disconcerting surprises began to emerge over a six-week period, making everyone hold their breath in anxious anticipation about what would happen between then and the birth of the child.

Let's review the facts of the case more closely and in chronological order.

On April 19th, 2001, Catherine underwent another sonogram to ascertain the sex of the child. Initially it was the nurse technician who performed the examination, but something strange emerged right away. The technician immediately called the physician directly responsible for the exam and who would sign the final results. According to practice in the United States, if something goes wrong, the physician is ultimately the one responsible. But things did not proceed as they should have. The physician kept Catherine's gynecologist, Lisa, informed of what was going on from the beginning. She told Lisa that the clinical report was not normal and asked that Catherine undergo a more detailed sonogram at a prenatal specialist on the following day. The physician, Carol, a specialist at the Megella Medical Group, oversaw the sonogram, and immediately noticed that there was virtually no amniotic fluid (*oligohydramnios*). At the same time, however, there was an abundance of liquid in the peritoneal cavity (*ascites*). It is well known that this condition can result in excessive pressure on the fetus's chest, limiting thoracic movements and consequently inhibiting pulmonary growth and development.

The medical team was unanimous in recommending further tests and was obliged to perform amniocentesis because of the lack of amniotic fluid. All that they were able to do, given the state of mother and child, was to perform a paracentesis with an intake of about 125 cubic centimeters of ascitic fluid.

After three days, Catherine underwent yet another sonogram. The situation had not changed. On the following day, a second sample of ascitic fluid was taken, this time at a volume of 160 cubic centimeters. On the following day, a sonogram revealed that fluid began to seep again, and the fetal bladder was swollen. They detected enlarged kidneys and ureters (bilateral hydronephrosis). The trained eyes of the specialists recognized right away what is called a "keyhole": a dilation of the posterior urethra and the bladder neck (urethral obstruction). At this point, Doctor Carol was finally able to give her definitive diagnosis. The clinical chart reveals the grim prognosis: Urethral obstruction with fetal expansion of the bladder, rupture of the bladder itself and leakage of urine from the bladder into the fetal peritoneal cavity. In the days to follow, the mother had to undergo a series of procedures to remove even more ascitic fluid, but it continued to form and accumulate nonetheless. It is not hard to imagine the stress this caused her, the sense of uncertainty and deep suffering about what was going to happen. A further consultation with specialists led to a recommendation that Catherine be transferred to a higher level of specialty care at the University of California at Irvine, where a certain Doctor Manuel, an outstanding specialist in the field, could give further advice about what to do. The visit and ensuing tests, however, only confirmed what had been diagnosed previously. Nothing had changed in the interim. The only new development was a worsening of the fetal bilateral hydronephrosis. Although he regretted it deeply, the specialist had no choice but to tell the mother that the child's condition was extremely grave. At the twenty-sixth week, severe trauma was detected for the future functioning of the child's kidneys and lungs. It was a grim prognosis.

In the light of these results, Catherine, together with her husband Steven, decided not to undergo any additional invasive procedures. There simply was no therapeutic means of treating this kind of pathology. Broken hearted, she knew all she could do was wait it out. The only path forward was to have a sonogram done every week to monitor the situation closely. Up until the thirtieth week, the situation remained just as grave as before. More than ten other specialists analyzed the situation to see if anything could be done. All of them, however, went away shaking their heads in despondency, absolutely sure no solution to the problem was in sight. One of them even said to Catherine, "If it was my baby, I would pray to God to allow him to die quickly." The situation was unbearable. The medical doctors were in continual consultation with one another, discussing various possible solutions, but unlike any textbook case they had seen before, this was entirely unique. They were facing a persistent, severe, and utter absence of amniotic fluid for a period of six weeks of gestation, in addition to the serious collateral effects associated therewith. Catherine was suffering deeply. She and Steven desperately wanted Elizabeth to have a little brother, and now everything seemed on the brink of collapse. Her own testimony is heart wrenching:

> The doctors told me that the bladder was extremely dilated and that the fluid was causing them the greatest concern because the child was not able to urinate; his kidneys were just not functioning. Our greatest worry was that the kidneys would never be able to function ... the

> kidneys refused to function ... the situation
> seemed quite desperate.

Catherine's suffering was shared not only by her husband Steve, but by her mother, relatives, and friends. The joy they had first felt at the possible birth of a second child turned into a nightmare. The future seemed to bode nothing but the death of the child at the moment of childbirth. In the best-case scenario, the child would have serious renal and pulmonary malformation, which in any case would eventually lead to death sooner or later. Someone had even suggested the possibility of abortion, but Catherine would hear nothing of it. Stephen, fully in agreement with his wife, also would not have considered that possibility. Granted, he was an unbeliever. His only certainties were those provided by science. He was convinced you cannot contradict science since science is the ultimate truth. Nonetheless, he would not accept abortion. It did not enter his field of vision, even as an unbeliever. All he could hope for was a medical solution. That was all he could depend on.

This is precisely where Sister Liliana came onto the scene. Sister Liliana is a Maltese Sister of the Institute "Holy Child Mary" and a good friend of the family. She went to visit Catherine when she had heard of the dire situation the mother was in. When Sister Liliana spoke with Catherine, she invited her to pray to Paul VI to ask for the grace of a happy end to her pregnancy. There was a reason Sister Liliana suggested Paul VI's name. She had known Pope Paul VI when he was Cardinal Archbishop of Milan. Since he was the Cardinal protector of their order, he would stay with them whenever he came to Rome. Her testimony is valuable and reveals

many significant personality traits of Paul VI, whom
she admired especially for his simplicity and generosity:

> When he was Cardinal Archbishop of Milan, he
> also served as Cardinal Protector of our Insti-
> tute. I was the personal secretary to Mother
> General at the time. He stayed with us often. I
> remember that I was still a novice at the time
> preparing to take my first vows in 1961. He was
> in town for the Senate of Bishops, staying in a
> private apartment at our Motherhouse. Some-
> times he would come and spend entire days in
> prayer at our house. He used to the go into the
> Chapel of "Holy Child Mary" and we would
> see him with open hands praying to the child
> Mary. One day, Mother General sent me to the
> guest room to see if the sister in charge of
> keeping it clean needed help. I was in the
> kitchenette getting a glass of water to drink and
> the Cardinal came out of a side door. I was a
> little surprised and he said to me, "Oh, who do
> we have here?" "I'm a novice," I responded. He
> asked me where I as from and whether my
> parents were still living. Then he said, "I'm
> thirsty too." I was frozen in my tracks and then
> realized he didn't want me to feel embarrassed.
> He continued to talk. He wanted to know what
> I was doing at the Mother House. He gave me
> his blessing, took my face in his hands and said,
> "Now remember: I am your Cardinal Protector
> and if you are in need of anything, you let me
> know." This is the reason I am telling you now
> to remember what he said to me. Later on,
> Mother General said to me, "The one who spoke
> to you today is the meek Christ on earth." And
> so every time he came to our Mother House to
> give a conference to the sisters, I was asked to
> translate into English so that the whole commu-

nity would understand what he was saying. So
that's how it was then … He also came once
when the Mother General was not there. She
was in India for Easter, and he arrived with his
secretary Msgr Macchi around 10:00 p.m. They
rang the bell and I went to answer the door.
Cardinal Montini had brought two boxes of
wine and two boxes of candy for the sisters.
Then he asked me to call the sisters. In his arms
he had a lamb with a red ribbon. He bade me
again to call the sisters even though it was
rather late. All of the sisters gathered in the
recreation room. He said, "I wanted to come.
Mother is gone so Father had to come because
this is the Paschal Feast." He loved those
moments. He usually went to the outskirts of
Milan to visit the poor and he didn't want
anyone to recognize that he was a Cardinal. All
these gestures are seared into my heart.

This direct knowledge of Paul VI allowed Sister Liliana
to spread word of the pope's holy life everywhere she
was called to exercise her apostolate. On this occasion,
however, she did not have her customary holy card
with the relics of Pope Montini. She promised to send
one to Catherine as soon as she got home. And she did.
As soon as she got back to the convent, she mailed
Catherine a holy card. But even this was not enough.
She herself began to pray to Paul VI asking that the life
of the child be saved. She has given direct testimony
of this. When asked about the precise content of her
prayer, she responded:

> To save the baby's life. I said it to them and I
> said it to myself: "What is impossible for man
> is possible for God. If God wants it, it will
> happen. If God does not want it, He has a

reason." That is my faith. As far as regards the prayer, I pray spontaneously to Paul VI as if I were speaking with him face-to-face: "You are so close to God, help us! Help Catherine and that baby. Show the truth to all those people who said she should have an abortion." We were really worried for her, as well as for the baby ... I was praying and hoping and wanting Paul VI to do something. That is how I was speaking with him.

The prayers of intercession to Pope Paul VI multiplied. The mother and grandmother of little George, the parish community, and many other people united their prayers to ask the pope of *Humanae Vitae* to allow George to be born healthy and safe.

Then suddenly, at the thirty-first week of pregnancy, there was a radical turn in every aspect of the pregnancy. The bladder returned to normal size and the amniotic fluid returned to a normal level. The kidneys, however, remained in such grave condition that the doctors predicted George would live no more than two days after birth. But the clinical conditions of the child improved and stabilized up until the time of birth, which occurred at the thirty-ninth week by a Caesarean section. From the moment of birth, George neither suffered nor showed any sign of respiratory difficulty, nor problems with his kidneys, nor any other symptoms associated with the pathology. He only had to undergo a minor treatment to repair a urethral valve. George was able to leave the hospital safe and sound, and at the moment Paul VI's cause was underway, he was twelve years old and perfectly healthy. Pope Paul VI heard the prayers raised up to him by so many people and watched over this tiny creature not only in the last stages of gestation, but also at the critical moment of birth.

Medical doctors tend to eschew the word "miracle." After all, it's only natural for them to stick to the knowledge they gain from medical science. A physician presents clinical data, the results of sonogram analysis, and anything else revealed by clinical examinations. The words of the stupefied gynecologist, therefore, best summarize the amazing events of those last weeks of gestation: "It was an absolute surprise. I had never seen a transformation like that. It was as if I were looking at an entirely different baby." The medical records, updated regularly after each new test, were analyzed carefully by the medical Commission assigned to the case. The questions the Commission needed to answer were straightforward. Four clear questions to which the members were expected to give equally clear answers. First of all, they had to confirm the diagnosis given at the time. The answer they gave was clear enough: "Grave stenosis of the urethral valve arising in the prenatal stage with associated bladder complications (microlesions with suspected rupture), bilateral hydronephrosis, oligohydramnios, urinary ascites, and probable pulmonary hypoplasia." The second question was in regard to the fetus' state of health. The medical doctors had determined it was "inauspicious." The third was in regard to the applied therapy. The specialists on the medical Commission ascertained that nothing more could have been done than what the American medical team had already done. In the prenatal stage, there simply was no effective therapy possible. The last question is always the most important. The Commission must make a judgment on the healing itself. Here was its lapidary response: the healing was "sudden, complete, and lasting, and not explicable according to current medical science." The consensus of the doctors is an assurance to the one presenting the case for beatification. After all, we must remember that the healing occurred in 2001 at a premier prenatal care facility in the United States where the medical technology is first class. The conclusion, therefore, was that Paul VI had heard the prayers of the faithful and acted as an intercessor before God to bring out this extraordinary sign of grace inexplicable by modern science.

CONCLUSION

HANKS TO HIS beatification, the Church can look upon Paul VI's sanctity with greater conviction. His life, teaching, and intimate bond with the Church on earth will be a sign to future generations of the Lord's fidelity as expressed to his disciples: "Amen, amen, I say to you, whoever believes in me will do the works that I do, and will do greater ones than these, because I am going to the Father" (Jn 14:12).

Paul VI stands strong as an outstanding example of holiness lived without shame or embarrassment. Even though he stood at the center of the Church, he offered an authentic witness of faith, hope, and love to the Church and to the world in an almost spontaneous way. Even though he lived life with unshakable loyalty and determination, he lived it in response to a gift he had received and a vocation for which he felt entirely responsible. The various facets of Paul VI's life converged in a daily commitment to perform the many demands of the Christian life in faith, hope, and love. The testimonies to his life unanimously affirm his sanctity. The very criticisms aimed at certain aspects of his leadership reveal not only his strength and decisiveness, but also his high respect for others as he strove to solve enormously complicated problems that seem so simple if one only sees a part of the problem or approaches them from only one angle.

Paul VI's example shines with particular brightness today. His intense, profound, and incisive teaching is especially prophetic today. His Eucharistic and Marian piety, his love for the liturgy and the Church's common prayer, his impartial love for the Church even in its most extreme moments of suffering, the sweet, sincere affability with which he treated everyone he met, and, finally, his full and complete dedication to Christ and His Church: all of this created in the People of God a deep conviction of his holiness.

Perhaps there is no better way to conclude these reflections on Pope Paul VI than with the words of his successor Pope St John Paul II:

> Paul VI was a *gift of the Lord to His Church*. As I said on the first anniversary of his death, the Holy Spirit had given him, and to John XXIII— so highly esteemed by both him and me—"the charism of transformation, thanks to which the figure of the Church, known to everyone, was shown to be both same and different." The Church, faithful to the Lord, always remains herself; but the Church, continually spurred on by her love for the Lord, never grows weary in the task of deepening her understanding of who she is. The more clearly she understands the divine plan and conforms herself to it, the more thoroughly she can be renewed and effectively carry out the mission entrusted to her by Christ. This in fact was the providential program of the Second Vatican Council, which Paul VI guided to its happy conclusion and of which he was the primary herald and implementer. We can never underestimate the problems and difficulties Paul VI had to face to ensure that the Church would not be undermined by a misunderstanding of "transformation." We can never

thank Christ the Lord enough for having chosen Paul VI to navigate the mystical barque of Peter at a time when waves were battering it on every side. Today we can see more clearly how deep his spirituality was, how far-sighted his vision, how bright his wisdom. His life stands as proof that there can be no "transformation" of the Church without personal sanctification. He taught us by his life and death how we should love Christ, how we should serve the Church, and how we must give ourselves for the salvation of all mankind. Paul VI was also *a gift of the Lord to humanity.* He understood modern man, loved him with a supernatural love: looking at him, that is, with the merciful eyes of Christ. Inaugurating the fourth session of the Council, which he called "a solemn act of love for humanity," he said, "again, and above all else, love: love for the men and women of today, whoever they are, wherever they are, and without exclusion." His intelligence and culture endowed him with an acute sense of the grandeur and poverty of man in the contradictory situation typical of our generation. But his faith and charity inspired him toward that "civilization of love" without which, today more than ever, it is difficult for man to find solutions to the problems that trouble him deeply. He understood man because he looked at him with the eyes of Christ. He helped man because he loved him with the love of Christ. He served man because he showed him the truth of Christ in all its fullness.

CPSIA information can be obtained
at www.ICGtesting.com
Printed in the USA
LVOW11s2327160217
524580LV00001B/31/P